HIDDEN GALWAY

ANCIENT GATEWAY, GALWAY.

R.15

WILLIAM HENRY

HIDDEN GALWAY

GALLOWS, GARRISONS AND GUTTERSNIPES

MERCIER PRESS

IRISH PUBLISHER – IRISH STORY

MERCIER PRESS

Cork

www.mercierpress.ie

© William Henry, 2011

© Foreword: Pat McMahon, 2011

ISBN: 978 1 85635 754 8

10 9 8 7 6 5 4 3 2 1

A CIP record for this title is available from the British Library

Printed and bound in the EU.

Contents

Lynch Memorial Stone, Galway

For Jacqueline

The real magic at the end of
the rainbow is deep spiritual
friendship

Acknowledgements

Thanks to the following people: my wife Noreen, sons Patrick and David, and daughter Lisa. My grateful appreciation to the National Library of Ireland, Dublin; the staff of the James Hardiman Library, NUIG: Michael Faherty, Marie Boran, Liam Frehan, Michael O'Connor, Geraldine Curtain, Anne Mitchell; County Galway Library, Island House: Maureen Moran and Mary Kavanagh. Thanks also to Shane O'Brien, Ciara Thornton and Lisa Henry for their help, and my grateful appreciation to the committee of the Galway Archaeological and Historical Society for the use of their invaluable journal and lecture series. With thanks also to the committee of the Old Galway Society for the use of their very valuable lecture series. Both societies are to be highly commended for the priceless work that they do, providing and promoting such a wealth of valuable information on the history and heritage of Galway.

Thanks also to all in the media: Galway Bay FM, Raidió na Gaeltachta, *The Connacht Tribune*, *The Tuam Herald*, the *Galway Advertiser* and the *Galway Independent*, including those who gave excellent publicity to this project: Declan Dooley, Hilary Martyn, Brendan Carroll, Dave Hickey, Joe O'Shaughnessy, Ronnie O'Gorman, Dickie Byrne, Éamonn Howley, Mark Kennedy, Tom Kenny, Keith Finnegan, Tom Gilmore, Jim Carney, Mary Conroy, Peadar O'Dowd, Des Kelly and Máirtín Tom Sheáinin.

William Henry

Special thanks also to Victoria Armst, Anne Maria Furey, Pamela O'Hanlon, Kieran Hoare, James Casserly, Marita Silke, Bob and Mary Waller, and Bill and Alice Scanlan for reading my work and making many valuable suggestions; also to Fionnulla Tarpy, Tommy Holohan, Eamon O'Regan and Norbert Sheerin. I am again deeply indebted to a very special friend, Jacqueline O'Brien, who has, as always, given so generously of her time, researching and proofreading, and for her expert advice, encouragement and support throughout this project. This book is dedicated to Jacqueline in appreciation for her years of commitment to research and for her extraordinary ability and enthusiasm in discovering the unknown and hidden histories of Galway.

Foreword

I t gives me great pleasure to contribute this foreword to William Henry's interesting and valuable book *Hidden Galway*, which he has so wonderfully subtitled *Gallows, Garrisons and Guttersnipes*. William has a great love of Galway, and a great understanding of the people of Galway, and it is this which allows him to bring history to readers and to audiences in a most meaningful and accessible way.

His writings excel in their conversational and engaging tone. In this book, as in his talks and lectures, William Henry brings joy, generosity and a wonderful spirit, allowing local history to tell us about ourselves. In reading this book you will discover that local history is the very essence of life. The light of humanity at its best is to be found in his expressive descriptions.

In celebrating this book it is worth noting what the Peruvian writer Mario Vargas Llosa had to say about the writing of books and the compiling of histories when he received the Nobel Prize for Literature in November 2010, at about the same time that William Henry was composing this book. Llosa reminded people that heroism and the epic are as possible in the present as in the time when Homer's *The Odyssey* and *The Iliad* were being written. 'I have always been fascinated,' Llosa said, 'to imagine the uncertain circumstances in which our ancestors, with the language that allowed them to communicate having just recently been born ... gathered around fires, began to tell stories and compile histories.' Llosa points out that this was 'a crucial moment in our destiny, because in those circles civilisation began'.

This book and the other writings of William Henry are in that tradition, part of that never interrupted process from the cave and the open fire to the modern apartment and the skyscraper. In that tradition, William Henry's skills as a historian and as a communicator, and as a writer and as an educator, are in abundant evidence throughout this book.

The *Gallows, Garrisons and Guttersnipes* of the subtitle aptly describe what we might call the prose poems or vignettes through which William Henry illustrates the many aspects of the history of Galway, from a Christmas morning tragedy of 1842 to the railway children who played out their adventures in the long tunnel of the old Galway to Clifden railway line. The rich heritage of Galway, often lying hidden within disparate archival collections and within the walls of old buildings, has been brought to life in this engaging history, which new audiences, future generations and students, still unfamiliar with the history of their own area, will find compelling.

The Irish novelist Colum McCann has written that 'the past is all around us: the universal is local, brick by stolen brick'. Whether writing about the Hole in the Wall pub in Eyre Street, the Prospect Hill reservoirs, Cooper's Cave near the Font Roundabout on the Tuam road, Menlo Castle or the Old County Infirmary, William Henry in this book allows us to discover and to see so much of the past which is still all around us.

Pat McMahon,
County Librarian, Galway

Introduction

*H*idden Galway is a voyage of discovery through the corridors of time where a wealth of material is just waiting to be explored. Captured in its pages is a hidden history of events and people from Galway that introduces the reader to a new concept of the history of the town, hinterland and its people. While Galway was granted city status in 1484, it is continually referred to as both a town and city in many publications, and I have used both terms throughout this book.

One can pick up and read *Hidden Galway* with ease and interest, exploring the stories which are not well known. There are accounts of disasters, including the Anach Cuain tragedy, in which nineteen people drowned; the loss of a KLM flight, which brought Galway to a standstill for over a week in 1958; and the Christmas morning heartbreak of 1842, when thirty-seven people lost their lives while attending mass. Also explored is the story of 'William from Galway', the man who is reputed to have sailed with Christopher Columbus on his voyage of discovery in 1492. Graphic accounts of murder and executions, such as the infamous Bodkin murders, when eleven people were brutally slain in a house of horrors in one night, are included. Bandits, highwaymen and smugglers are also part of this hidden history, as are scientists and men and women of vision. There are stories of romance, which include the passionate interlude between Wolfe Tone and Elizabeth Martin of Dangan. The love story of Michael Bodkin and Nora Barnacle (wife of James Joyce) is told with great affection. One can follow Galwaymen fighting in foreign wars – men like Captain Martin Kirwan, a hero of the Franco-Prussian War. The tale of the O'Flaherty Rent will help bring some understanding to the old Galway saying 'May God preserve us from the ferocious O'Flahertys.' The life of an extraordinary blind piper, Martin Reilly, is examined. A brief look at the Knights Templar in Galway takes one back to an age of chivalry and betrayal. The story of the Italian Madonna of the Rosary now housed in the Claddagh church is told, and visitors to Galway, such as Tom 'The Moor' Molineaux, an African–American champion boxer who fought his way to freedom, and St Oliver Plunkett are brought to life. Those interested in sports can look forward to reading about the 'Great Marathon of the West' and its outstanding champion, Tom Hynes of Newcastle. Daniel O'Connell addressing a monster meeting at the Sliding Rock in Shantalla takes one back to a very difficult period in our history. The Emily Anderson story outlines the life of an exceptional woman who achieved so much abroad, without being well known in her home town of Galway. It is impossible to mention all of the stories in this introduction as there are so many subjects covered. Suffice it to say that while this book contains a serious history, there is also a light-hearted side to it, with something for everyone.

It was a pleasure to write this book as there were such a variety of subjects from which to choose. Over many years Jacqueline O'Brien, my co-researcher, and I had collated a wealth of information on various aspects of Galway. Much of this was collected while researching other books, when it was inevitable that we would find other interesting material. At times we became very distracted from the primary target of the research, so we simply amassed all of the information that we found interesting. Over time a huge file built up; however, we were unsure of how this material would be used. So you can imagine our delight when Mercier Press approached me with the idea of publishing a hidden history of Galway. The only problem in writing this book was not so much which stories to use, but rather which ones to leave out. The stories and accounts of Galway and its people contained in these pages only form a portion of the information we gathered.

The subtitle of the book, *Gallows, Garrisons and Guttersnipes*, was chosen for the following reasons. Firstly, there were a number of gallows located in Galway, the main one being at Eyre Square in front of the town gates. Public hangings were part of everyday life in old Galway and continued behind jail walls in the late nineteenth century. Secondly, over the years Galway was often referred to as a 'garrison town'. Many people believe this was due to Renmore Barracks opening in 1880, but there was a military presence in Galway from the earliest times. Finally, the word 'guttersnipe' was used during a court case in the nineteenth century by a judge when passing sentence on a number of young individuals who found themselves before him, having been caught causing a nuisance in the town. The word is still used from time to time to describe youngsters causing minor problems.

Hidden Galway is also a treasure for collectors as it forms part of a very important series of publications that is opening up Irish history and sharing valuable information with the public. Many of these stories had not been fully investigated before this publication, which makes them extremely important, as they have helped shape the modern city. This journey through the uncharted waters of Galway's past will be, in many respects, a revelation to the public and indeed to some historians. It is ideal for those who prefer a short history of events and people rather than comprehensive studies of a particular subject. It will also be of great value to Irish communities abroad and indeed those with an interest in Irish history. To quote one historian who read the manuscript, 'It's a book for those who wish to know everything about Galway and more.'

William Henry, 2011

Galway – What's in a name?

For centuries, people have wondered about the origins of the name Galway. The nineteenth-century historian James Hardiman states that the little village that existed near the mouth of the River Corrib before the arrival of the Normans was called Ballinshruane, meaning 'the town of the little streams'. Another tradition informs us that the ancient Irish called all foreigners '*gall*', and when the Norman settlers arrived in the area they were called *Clan-na-Gall*, meaning 'foreign clan'. This could clarify at least part of the name *Gal*-way.

According to Cuchoigcriche Ó Cléirigh, one of the Four Masters (authors of a seventeenth-century chronicle of Irish history called *The Annals of the Kingdom of Ireland* or *Annals of the Four Masters*), the town took its name from the River Gaillimh, named after a Fir Bolg princess who drowned there. Gaillimh was the daughter of a chieftain named Breasail, whose name is sometimes associated with the Irish mythical island of Hy-Brasil. In some traditions the mythical Tír na nÓg, the Land of Eternal Youth, is linked with this island.

There is an old story about Spanish sailors who went in search of Hy-Brasil. According to the legend, the island always remained just out of their reach. Try as they might to land on its enchanted shores, it would fade before their eyes. The sailors did not fully realise just how far they had journeyed, but before returning home they sighted a huge landmass and upon landing there named that place Brasil, now known as Brazil. Thus, some folklorists say that the father gave his name to Brazil while the daughter gave her name to Galway.

While all of this is legend, the seventeenth-century historian Sir James Ware tells us that the town of Galway may have taken its name from the River Galvia – which could be a variation of Gaillimh – as mentioned in the *Annals of Roscommon* in 1177 and 1190. The celebrated seventeenth-century historian Roderic O'Flaherty agrees that the town takes its name from the river. Others believe that Gaillimh is a name derived from two words 'gall' and 'amh', indicating a stony river, which is visible during low tide at the river mouth.[1] Today, this watercourse is called the River Corrib, taking its name from Lough Corrib. Corrib is a derivation of its ancient name, Lough Orbsen. According to legend, Orbsen was a member of the Tuatha de Danaan, a mythological Irish race who lived here many centuries ago.[2]

While all of these theories are worth noting, the true origin of the name Galway is now lost to antiquity.

There is also a tradition in Galway that because the ancient town had fourteen streets, lanes, towers and tribes it was modelling itself on Rome, but doubled up on the 'eternal

---

1   J. Hardiman, *The History of the Town and County of the town of Galway* (Galway: facsimile of 1820 edition, *The Connacht Tribune*, 1985).

2   R. O'Flaherty (edited by J. Hardiman), *A Chorographical Description of West or H-Iar Connaught, Galway 1684* (Dublin: The Irish Archaeological Society, 1846).

city', thus making it twice as important. The following poem appeared in *The Connacht Tribune* in 1910. It had no title and the author was unknown:

> Galway – Cannacion Rome – twice equals those
> She boasts twice seven illustrious families;
> Twice seven towers defend her lofty walls
> And polished marble decks her splendid halls.
> Twice seven her massive gates, o'er which arise
>
> Twice seven strong castles towering to the skies;
> Twice seven her bridges, thro' those arches flow
> The silvery tides, majestically slow.
> Her ample church, with twice seven altars flames;
> As heavenly patron every altar claims.[3]

Sunday Boy Blake

This is the story of Sir Valentine Blake or, as he was more popularly known, 'Sunday Boy Blake'. He was descended from one of the old tribal families of Galway and lived in Menlo Castle on the banks of the River Corrib. Blake, one of the well-known characters of nineteenth-century Galway, was in the habit of neglecting his financial responsibilities and was seldom out of debt. Because of this, he could not leave the confines of his castle, as therein his creditors and the authorities could not serve him a summons

---

3   'The City of the Tribes', *The Connacht Tribune*, 31 December 1910.

for the monies he owed. It seems that they could not serve the summons on a Sunday either, and consequently Valentine Blake made full use of this loophole in the law.[4] The County Club, now the Hibernian House, was a social club for the landed gentry and the professional classes at that time. On Sunday mornings Blake would ride there to meet with friends and wine and dine all day.[5] However, he had to be careful – he had to be inside the gates of his castle before midnight. As the critical hour approached, he would mount his horse or get into his carriage and make his way to Menlo. There were many occasions when he cut the timing very close and had to gallop his horse at great speed, with the sheriff and bailiffs in hot pursuit. These actions earned him the name 'Sunday Boy Blake' and his escapades became known as the Menlo Race. His antics were a source of great entertainment for the local people and when they heard the sound of the galloping horses thundering past their homes they would say that Sunday Boy Blake was abroad again.

Despite being well under the influence of alcohol, Sunday Boy always made it through the outer gates before the midnight hour, much to the annoyance of his pursuers and to the delight of the local people. At some point during this period he became aware of another loophole in the law, which specified that Members of Parliament were exempt from being served with a financial writ. He decided to seek election and ran his campaign from Menlo Castle. Blake

4   P. O'Dowd, 'Walking Tour of Old Galway', City Tour Leaflet, Galway, 1 March 1992.

5   P. O'Dowd, *Old and New Galway* (Galway: The Archaeological, Historical & Folklore Society and *The Connacht Tribune*, 1985), p. 83.

canvassed for votes from a boat at Woodquay, as he discovered that writs could not be served on water either. He was elected as an MP for Galway in 1841 amid great acclaim. Sunday Boy Blake died in 1847 during the height of the famine.[6]

The Justice Stone

There is a large stone located in a field on the old Oranmore to Galway road that has been identified as a boulder tomb or dolmen dating from the Irish Neolithic period, *c.* 3000 BC. It is known locally as the Justice Stone. During the nineteenth century a judge is reputed to have passed judgement from the stone when delayed by flooding en route to Galway. The judge had been asked to settle a serious dispute between two local men. Both men, who were unable to swim, had been either fishing or sailing out on Galway Bay when one of them accidentally fell overboard. The other man, in an attempt to save his companion, pitched him the only 'lifeline' he had, which was a length of fishing tackle containing hooks. The man grabbed the fishing tackle and was pulled to safety. However, during the rescue, the hooks injured him. Some said that he lost an eye. The rescued man later decided to sue his rescuer for damages. The judge asked the rescuer if he could have saved the man without using the fishing tackle. The man

---

6   O'Dowd, 'Walking Tour of Old Galway'.

replied 'No', saying that the fishing tackle was all that was available to him. The judge then reminded the plaintiff that his life had been saved and asked him to re-consider his course of action: after all, he would otherwise be dead! The plaintiff replied by saying that he could possibly have made it back to the boat without help, thus saving himself.

The judge sat upon the Justice Stone and considered the situation. Some time passed before he came to a decision. There was, he said, only one way to settle this dispute: both men would have to go back out in the boat and when they reached the area where the incident had occurred the plaintiff would have to jump into the sea. The judge told the rescuer that he could not interfere with the man in the water, who, if he were able to reach the boat without drowning, would win the case. If he drowned, the other man would be justified. The plaintiff declined to take part in the exercise and so the rescuer won the case. Some say that afterwards the judge would make a point of stopping at the Justice Stone on his way to Galway and settle other local disputes.[7]

The story is interesting in that it has similarities to the biblical story of Solomon's wisdom and the two women who both claimed to be the mother of the same baby. To settle the dispute, Solomon ordered one of his soldiers to cut the baby in half, thus dividing the infant between both women. Upon hearing his orders, one of the women called out in horror, saying the other woman could have the baby. Solomon then ordered the soldier to give the baby to the

---

7   W. Henry, 'The Justice Stone', *St Patrick's Parish Magazine* 2010, pp. 7–8.

woman who had cried out, saying that only the real mother would give up her baby rather than see the child killed.

There is another version of the story, which names the monument as the 'Judge's Stone'. A judge was on his way to Galway by coach to preside over the case, as above. He stopped near the stone to await his escort into Galway, and while waiting he noticed some children playing on the stone. The judge left the coach, approached the children and asked about the game they were playing. They replied 'It's "Court", your honour,' and told him they were trying the case he was on his way to preside over in Galway. The judge was amused and asked his young 'counterpart' what his verdict would be.

'The man ought to be taken to the same place and thrown into the sea again, and if he is able to save himself without the fishing line, he is to get compensation, but if not, he has to lose it.'

The judge was very impressed and passed down the same verdict in court later that day.[8]

The Menlo Dolmen

The first indication of permanent settlement in the Galway area is a dolmen, more commonly known as

---

8   B. Furey, *The History of Oranmore Maree* (Galway: Brenda Furey, 1991), p. 113.

a portal tomb. It is situated on land overlooking Lough Corrib, near Menlo village. A dolmen was a burial place, mainly for the cremated bodies of the Neolithic people who lived in Ireland around 3000 BC. These people began clearing the forests for farming, which resulted in an improved diet and way of life. Through extensive farming, food could be stored, thus allowing these people time to explore their surroundings and produce early pottery and tools.

Additional evidence of these early farmers was found on the bed of the River Corrib during the 1970s. Artefacts included examples of stone axe-heads, arrowheads and other implements used by this early agricultural community. The Menlo dolmen is possibly the oldest structure in Galway, yet it is practically unknown.[9]

The O'Flaherty Rent

There are many stories told about the famous O'Flaherty clan of Galway. One of these stories is known as the O'Flaherty Rent. During the sixteenth century the main O'Flaherty stronghold was Aughnanure Castle near Oughterard. At the time, the only way for the native Irish to hold on to their land was to submit to the king or queen

---

9   P. Gosling, *Archaeological Inventory of County Galway, Volume 1: West Galway* (Dublin: The Stationery Office, 1993), p. 11.

of England, but this meant taking the Oath of Supremacy (swearing allegiance to the monarch as Supreme Governor of the Church of England). Once the oath was taken, the land would be re-granted to them, but in many cases a rent had to be paid to an overlord appointed by the authorities. The O'Flaherty chief agreed to pay the rent to the de Burgos in Terryland Castle, which was situated on the east bank of the River Corrib, just outside the city. The ruins of this castle are located close to the present Quincentennial Bridge.

It seems that three years went by without O'Flaherty paying any rent. De Burgo decided it was time to collect the money owed to him and sent his son to Aughnanure Castle to demand payment. The young man made his way to the O'Flaherty stronghold and asked to speak with the chieftain. As it happened, there was banquet being held in the castle when young de Burgo arrived, and he was invited to join in the merriment. He accepted the invitation and was given a place of prominence at the table, seated close to the O'Flaherty chief. He was royally treated and given a selection of rich foods, washed down by jugs of wine, while at the same time being entertained by musicians and singers.

As the night wore on, de Burgo raised the issue of the rent owed to his father. The O'Flaherty chieftain went silent and after a few moments said, 'Is it payment you want?' Before the young man could reply, O'Flaherty added, 'Sure I have it for you under my foot.'

Suddenly a trap door opened in the floor beneath de Burgo and he disappeared from the banqueting room without even being noticed. The trap door was known as the 'Flag Stone of Treachery'. There was a river running beneath the banqueting hall, and this was where de Burgo landed. O'Flaherty sent his men down after him and once they located him they cut his head off and placed it in a sack, then mounted their horses and rode to Terryland Castle. At the time the river could easily be crossed on horseback when the water was low. As the men crossed the river in the semi-darkness of that moonlit night, a sentry called out, asking who was approaching the castle and what business they were pursuing.

'It is the O'Flahertys from Aughnanure,' one of them replied, and tossed the sack at the sentry's feet, adding, 'If it's rent your master is looking for from the O'Flahertys, there it is at your feet, paid with interest and arrears.'

They turned their horses and rode back to Aughnanure. The sentry grabbed the sack, took it to his master and explained how the O'Flahertys had at last paid the rent. At first de Burgo was pleased, but then wondered about his son and why had he not returned with the rent himself. Upon opening the sack, de Burgo cried out in horror at the sight of his son's head.[10]

According to the story, de Burgo became extremely fearful for his own safety and that of his remaining family and decided to move away from Terryland. He had a small castle built a few miles away from the river. However, he only lived in the castle for one day because that night he had a dream that the O'Flahertys crossed the river with all their forces and beheaded him and the rest of his family. Such was his

---

10   R. Hayward, *The Corrib Country* (Dundalk: Dundalgan Press, 1968), pp. 153–5.

fear that he moved away from the area entirely and built a castle at Portumna, where he felt safe.

Shortly afterwards, the small castle became known as *Cashlain an Gar*, meaning the 'Short Castle', or the castle of the short stay. The area has since become known as Castlegar. The banqueting hall at Aughnanure Castle where the terrible deed was committed has since disappeared, but the remains of its outer wall can still be seen, and the river where young de Burgo lost his head still flows.[11]

Graves in Merlin Woods

There are a number of theories regarding the origins of the townland name of Doughiska (west Galway city). Some believe the name derives from the Irish for 'black water' or 'pool'. However, as with other place names throughout Ireland, the folklore is often more interesting and exciting.

According to one legend, the name Doughiska is derived from the murder of an old couple who lived in Merlin woods and had an inn there during Cromwellian times. The story goes that in 1650 an advance party of the Cromwellian army stopped in the area on their way to Galway city. Some of the soldiers went into the inn and asked for a drink of water. The old couple, being Gaelic speakers, did not understand

---

11   W. Henry, 'The O'Flaherty Rent', Information Leaflet, Galway, 2010.

the soldiers' request and so did not respond. The soldiers in turn did not understand the Irish language and, believing that they were being refused water, they were infuriated. They killed the couple and buried them in the woods. Another version of the story suggests that the soldiers were looking for alcohol and the old couple thought it was a drink of water they were requesting. Over time the story was passed down through generations of local people and the legend grew that the couple were killed for a drink of water, hence this darker interpretation of the name Doughiska. There are two memorial stones located in the grounds of Merlin Park Hospital close to the woods, reputed to mark the graves of the old couple.[12] There is also a portion of a wall and some stone steps close by, which are believed to be the remains of the inn.

However, the problem with this legend is that this area was known as Doughiska long before the Cromwellians arrived in Ireland. In fact, it is mentioned as early as 1383.[13] Nevertheless, the memorial stones in Merlin Park are very interesting. One of them is 2 metres long while the other is a few centimetres longer. Both are less than a metre wide and about 15 centimetres in thickness. The larger stone is inscribed with a cross and carvings, which R. A. S. Macalister (the nineteenth-century antiquarian writing for the Royal Society of Antiquaries of Ireland) described as the tools of a blacksmith: a bellows, knife and shoeing stone. He also identified its inscription as 'Conor

12 N. Sheerin, 'Ancient Graves in Merlin Park', *Frankly Speaking*, Western Heath Board Newsletter, Galway, 2002, p. 18.
13 M. L. Athy and H. Hodgson, 'Notes on the Ordnance Survey Letters', *Journal of the Galway Archaeological & Historical Society*, 8, no. 3, 1913–14, p. 152.

O'Reillie 1650'. The smaller stone is inscribed with a cross only. Their position is also interesting, given that they were recorded as being located close to where 'a high road once ran'.[14] This could possibly refer to *Bóthar na Caillighe*, the old road that once ran through Doughiska.

St Augustine's Well

The holy well located on the seashore along Lough Atalia Road has a history dating back centuries. It is known today as St Augustine's Well, but many such sites have pagan origins. In Ireland religious cults associated with water date from at least the late Bronze Age. Although wells or holy wells appear to be Christian monuments, much of the ritual, folklore and indeed the very preoccupation with water as a medium for supernatural cures displays strong pre-Christian elements. Many of the ancient rituals associated with these places disappeared during the early Christian period.[15] It has been suggested that rather than destroy these sites and prevent people from worshipping there, the early missionaries simply 'Christianised' them. They became holy wells and over time were given saints' names.

As the name suggests, St Augustine's Well takes its name

---

14 *Ibid.*
15 'Holy Wells' in Gosling, *Archaeological Inventory of County Galway* , p. 116.

from the Augustinian friars who built an abbey close by, on Forthill *c.* AD 1500. In the past the well was visited by large numbers of people, particularly on 28 August, St Augustine's feast day. Like other such sites, the well was associated with cures for certain ailments. On 11 June 1673 an extraordinary 'recovery' or cure occurred at St Augustine's Well. Patrick Lynch claimed to have experienced healing from what seems to have been a serious stomach complaint. There was an inquiry into the case at the time and eleven prominent men of the town signed as witnesses to the findings on 23 June 1673. Another witness, Mary Burke, believed that the cure was of a miraculous nature. In the official report words like 'miraculous', 'cure' and 'vision' were replaced with more cautious words like 'extraordinaire', 'amendment' and 'seen by him'. Those on the commission of inquiry would not commit themselves by claiming that a miracle had taken place and left the case open for a more natural explanation, which never materialised.[16]

The well continued to be a place of devotion for centuries. In more recent tradition, people visited and worshipped there annually on the last Sunday of July and the first Sunday in August. There were two other wells in the area, but these have since disappeared. The nineteenth-century historian James Hardiman recorded that the water from this well was noted for several cures, in particular for restoring vision. There is also a tradition of people dropping coins into the well, but it is not known when this custom began. It

---

16   W. Henry, *Role of Honour: The Mayors of Galway City 1485–2001* (Galway: Galway City Council, 2001), p. 89.

was sometimes referred to as St Colmcille's Well by the old Claddagh people, but there may be some confusion with one of the other wells that no longer exist.[17]

By the late 1990s the well had fallen into a ruinous state. The Galway Civic Trust carried out restoration work on it and the immediate surrounding area in 2000. St Augustine's Well is still visited by many people throughout the year.

Mutton Island Lighthouse

The earliest-known sea-light in Ireland, and probably in the British Isles, was at Hook Head, County Wexford. During the fifth century St Dubhan from Wales settled there. Continuous high winds, gales and treacherous seas meant shipwrecks were all too common in the area. St Dubhan had a large iron basket suspended from a mast near the cliff's edge and kept a fire burning there all year round to help ships avoid trouble. Following his death, his followers continued this practice for another six centuries. A Norman tower was later built on the site and provided light for shipping. Similarly, the old castle on Mutton Island, which no longer exists, may have been utilised to provide light for vessels coming into Galway Bay.

---

17   B. A. Geoghegan, 'St Augustine's Holy Well', *Renmore Seagull*, vol. 3, no. 2, May 1998, p. 10.

Mutton Island takes its name from the flocks of sheep that were kept there, and has had a somewhat violent past. During the mid-seventeenth century Cromwellian troops occupied the island. The Irish commander, Bryan Roe O'Neill, leading 300 men, attacked the island, killed almost the entire garrison and captured much of their munitions. At that time there was some form of watchtower and a crude beacon on Mutton Island, which served as a lighthouse.

Prior to the nineteenth century some families made a good living from shipwrecks all around the coast of Ireland. These were not all the result of natural disasters: people would lure unsuspecting ships on to rocks – the use of misleading beacons proved particularly effective. The ships were then relieved of their valuable cargos. There is a tradition that these 'land pirates' lured one of the Spanish Armada ships to its doom near Barna. However, with the development of official lighthouses, such practices gradually died out.[18]

All lighthouses in Ireland were in private ownership until c. 1704, but from 1810 the building and maintenance of these structures was transferred to the Ballast Board of Dublin.[19] In June 1815 the Corporation's Inspector of Lighthouses, a Mr Halpin, was instructed to build a proper lighthouse in Galway, as funds had been made available.[20] The Mutton Island lighthouse went into operation on 25 October 1817.

---

18 P. Witington, 'Keepers of the Flame', *Cara* (Aer Lingus), vol. 28, no. 6, November–December 1995, p. 20.

19 B. Scanlan, 'Lighthouses – A Different Perspective', *Journal of the Galway Family History Society: Galway Roots - Clanna na Gaillimhe*, vol. 2, 1994, p. 61.

20 'The Light on Mutton Island', *Galway Advertiser*, 9 June 1994.

The first lighthouse keeper was Walter Walsh.

While this period is considered the golden age of lighthouses, they could be places of solitude and isolation. However, Mutton Island was located close to the old Claddagh village and to Galway city. It could be reached on foot during low tide, but a boat was otherwise required. Living accommodation was provided for the lighthouse keeper and his family. The land adjacent to the structure was cultivated and tilled, making the family self-sufficient. Seaweed was used as fertiliser and an assortment of shellfish from the shoreline around the island was eaten and utilised by them.[21]

By the nineteenth century the Commissioners of Irish Lights was established, and later became the Lighthouse Authority for Ireland. Discipline in lighthouses was strict. They were run in the same manner as any naval establishment, with daily logs being kept.[22] In November 1892 a new light was installed on Mutton Island, replacing the old fixed white light. The new light gave three seconds of light followed by three seconds of darkness. This was followed by eleven seconds of light and again three seconds of darkness.[23]

In 1923 the keeper received permission to keep a small boat at the lighthouse to ensure that his children could attend school. Later that year, because of the dangers of high winds and rough seas, the Irish Lights' board granted him

21   'To the Lighthouse', *Galway Advertiser*, 31 March 1994.
22   Scanlan, 'Lighthouses', p. 61.
23   'The Light on Mutton Island'.

an educational allowance to send the children to a boarding school in Galway. The lighthouse keeper was Thomas Scanlan; his son Bill later gave thirty-nine dedicated years to the service.[24] On 28 November 1958 the lighthouse on Mutton Island was automated and sadly the era of lighthouse keepers ended in Galway. The last keeper was J. J. McCann.

The light from Mutton Island was finally extinguished in 1977 when a floating, lighted buoy was set in place in Galway Bay. In 1999, after much controversy, Mutton Island was finally joined to the mainland by a causeway in order to provide Galway city with a sewage treatment plant.

Lighthouses were once the only lifeline for sailors on dark and dangerous nights. However, modern maritime technology has made many lighthouses throughout Ireland obsolete. While the Mutton Island lighthouse is now off-limits to the public, it can be visited during heritage week every year. Much restoration work has been carried out, returning this important structure to its former glory.

The Spanish Armada of 1588

There is a plaque, now almost covered with ivy, located on the wall of Forthill Cemetery commemorating a very brutal event in the history of Galway. In 1588 twenty-

---

24 'To the Lighthouse'.

five ships of the great Spanish Armada – which was the culmination of a long series of hostilities between King Philip II of Spain and Queen Elizabeth I of England – were destroyed in stormy weather off the west coast of Ireland.

The Spanish Armada consisted of 259 sailing crafts of various types. On board were 19,000 soldiers, 8,000 sailors and 2,000 oarsmen, who were chained to their oars. There were 1,545 volunteers, including 300 adventurers, 180 priests and monks, and 200 Irishmen. On 30 July 1588 the Armada entered the English Channel in perfect formation. It was an imposing sight, forming a seven-mile crescent across the horizon. The English fleet, under the command of Lord High Admiral Charles Howard of Effingham, Vice-Admiral Sir Francis Drake and Rear Admiral Sir John Hawkins, met them. The battle raged for a number of days, with the fiercest fighting taking place off Gravelines in the Spanish Netherlands. By 10 August the Spanish were defeated and the remaining ships of the great Armada were sailing for home via the North Atlantic. The loss of life for the Spanish at this stage was about 9,000 men, and sixty of their ships had been destroyed.

Before setting sail from Spain, the Commander-in-Chief of the Armada, the Duke of Medina Sidonia, had warned his men that if anything should go wrong with their plans they were to avoid the west coast of Ireland at all costs. However, on 16 September a fierce storm forced some of the fleeing fleet towards land and they foundered there. A number of the ships were lost off the Connemara coast, one close to Barna. It is estimated that 6,000–7,000 men lost their lives off the Irish west coast. Another 1,000 who had survived the ravages of the sea were put to the sword. Some 300 Spaniards who escaped were given refuge in Connemara. However, when the authorities became aware that Spanish soldiers were being given shelter by the local people, Sir Richard Bingham, governor of Connacht, issued orders that these men were to be handed over on 'pain of death'.[25] On being taken prisoner, over 300 Spanish soldiers were marched into Galway and taken directly to Forthill, overlooking the town and Galway Bay. No mercy was shown to them and all were brutally executed. The man responsible for the executions was Sir William FitzWilliam, Lord Deputy of Ireland, and he was present to ensure that his orders were carried out. Also present were some Augustinian friars who administered the last rites to the unfortunate prisoners.[26] A huge pit was dug to accommodate the bodies of the executed.

There is a tradition in Galway that two of the Spaniards escaped and eventually made their way back to Spain. Another account indicates that one Spanish soldier escaped and made his way to the island of Inchagoill on Lough Corrib and lived there for the remainder of his life. During the 1950s the skeletal remains of some of the victims were excavated on the north side of the present Forthill Cemetery (which had once formed part of the old burial ground) by the CIE railway company when carrying out some work.[27]

---

25   C. Purcell, 'The Armada: How the Spanish Armada Fell upon the West Coast of Ireland A.D. 1588 – Part 1', *Journal of the Westport Historical Society, Cathair na Mart*, vol. 4, no. 1, 1984, pp. 3–19.

26   P. O'Dowd, *Galway City* (Galway: Galway Corporation, 1998), p. 13.

27   'The Augustinians of Abbey Hill or Forthill, Galway', *Brat Muire/The Mantle*, no. 46, 1969, pp. 12–13.

This was a brutal episode in Galway's history, and one which should not be forgotten. On 22 June 1988 the Spanish Navy Marines corps, which was founded in Spain in 1537 and is the oldest marine corps in the world, commemorated the 400th anniversary of this terrible event by erecting a plaque at Forthill in memory of those executed. Members arrived at Galway docks dressed in the sixteenth-century uniforms of the Spanish soldiers, yellow tunic-shirts and breastplates. Pascual Barberan of the Spanish Navy Marines thanked and paid tribute to the people of Galway, particularly the women all those centuries ago, for the kindness shown to their soldiers. When the order was given, they hoisted their banners and marched in military formation to Forthill for the ceremony. The memorial plaque bears the Cross of St James and records the burial of the Spanish soldiers in Spanish followed by a blessing in Irish.

The 1816 Crosses

This is the term widely used in Galway to describe a series of small crosses carved onto a number of nineteenth-century buildings around the city. Some of them also have the IHS monogram (a combination of Greek letters representing the name Jesus Christ) and a date carved into the stone. In some examples, the person responsible has also carved his name: I (Latin for J) Healy. While they are termed

1816 crosses, they range in date throughout that decade, but most are dated between 1814 and 1819. It is not known how or why they originated, but it has been suggested that the 1816 crosses mark the laying of the foundation stone of the old pro-cathedral in 1816. This was the first Catholic church erected in Galway since the introduction of the Penal Laws in 1695. In fact, it was erected while some of these laws were still in place, as Catholic Emancipation was only granted in 1829. The remains of this building are located on the corner of Abbeygate Street Lower and Middle Street.

Galway Court House opened in 1815, and sometime later two of these '1816' carvings appeared on the facade of the building. They are located on each of the 'hue and cry' notice sections and while the name 'I Healy' appears on one of them, it was not fully completed. Perhaps the 'culprit' was apprehended in the process.[28]

Another interesting example appears on a four-foot-six-inch stone incorporated into the rear wall of a house at Menlo. This is inscribed with the date 1815 and the name I Healy.[29]

It is believed that there are over twenty examples of these carvings throughout Galway city. Some of the locations include College Road, the Spanish Arch, Druid Lane, the Grammar School, the Court House and Salthill, to name but a few.

---

28   O'Dowd, *Old and New Galway*, pp. 108–9.
29   P. O'Laoi, *History of Castlegar Parish* (Fr Padraic O'Laoi, 1998), p. 120.

Siena Tiles

S iena tiles can still be found over the front doors of houses in Galway city. These are small square blue and yellow tiles that bear the IHS monogram surrounded by a circle of flaming rays. A Franciscan priest, Fr Francis Donnelly, introduced them to Galway following a retreat for the Poor Clare nuns in 1913. Fr Donnelly preached on the power of the Holy Name, as advocated by the Franciscan St Bernadine of Siena during the fifteenth century. St Bernadine had promoted Jesus using the IHS monogram, the Greek form of the Holy Name. It is not surprising that during the early part of the twentieth century the Franciscans, especially the Third Order (men and women who have ordinary professions but who live a life of dedicated service to God through prayer, study and work), were the main impetus behind the devotion to the Siena tiles in Galway.[30]

Fr Donnelly believed that he could curtail the problem of drunkenness. It occurred to him that if he could persuade families to dedicate their homes to the Sacred Heart, this would go a long way in promoting his teachings. The families who agreed had a Siena tile inserted over their doorway as a public sign that they had invoked the blessing and protection of God on the house by dedicating the dwelling to the Sacred Heart. Although the Great War of 1914–18 was raging,

---

30   P. Walsh, *Discover Galway* (Dublin: O'Brien Press, 2001), pp. 111–12.

Fr Donnelly managed to procure a large quantity of tiles. Devotion quickly spread in the towns and cities where the Franciscans had established churches, and the tiles were in use up to about 1920.[31] There was a short revival during the 1930s, when additional tiles were erected.

There is a lot of contradictory information regarding the tiles, which are sometimes mistaken for Eucharistic tiles.[32] Their manufacture by the Franciscan Sisters of Siena has continued to present times. In Galway, the tiles were made available at the Franciscan Church in St Francis Street, and they were also available in some local shops.[33] The tiles can be found in many other parts of Ireland, including Ennis, Roscrea, Athlone and Sligo, but the colours and forms can vary from place to place. Siena tiles in Galway can be found in Bowling Green, Abbeygate Street and a number of other streets around the city.

Bollingbrook Fort

The remains of Bollingbrook fort are located close to Seán Mulvoy Road. The fort dates from the mid-seventeenth century and was constructed and occupied by

---

31 J. Higgins, *Christian Symbolism and Iconography in Ireland* (forthcoming).

32 'A View from the Canal, 1903', *Galway Advertiser*, 25 September 1997.

33 Higgins, *Christian Symbolism*.

the Cromwellian troops who were laying siege to Galway at the time. On 8 July 1651, Sir Charles Coote, lord president of Connacht and commander of the Cromwellian forces, arrived at the gates of Galway city and demanded its immediate surrender. The city refused and the people braced themselves for the consequences of that decision. The enemy troops immediately began to seal off the approaches to the town and a nine-month siege began. The troops constructed a rampart of earth stretching from Lough Atalia over the hill at Bohermore down to the Sandy River, along which they erected three star-shaped forts. One fort was located close to the present-day Moneenageisha junction; another larger fort stood on the site now occupied by the New Cemetery at Bohermore. The third fort, Bollingbrook, was erected on the slope of a hill leading down to the Sandy River. Only the eastern section of this fort has survived above ground and consists of an external ditch and two poorly preserved bastions. The overall length of the structure is 32 metres. The three forts and military ramparts that connected them are depicted in the famous 1651 pictorial map of Galway.

As the siege continued, supplies in the town dwindled. The problem was compounded by the increase in population in the months before the siege, as an influx of refugees had been driven before the Cromwellian armies. Two ships failed to run the blockade with supplies for the beleaguered city, and hunger within led to desperate measures to obtain food. In one attempt to drive cattle into the town, more than sixty people were killed by enemy fire from the troops occupying fortified positions. Throughout the winter of 1651 conditions steadily worsened and this continued into the spring of 1652, by which time Galway was the last city in Ireland and England holding out against the forces of Cromwell. With no hope of raising the siege and under the threat of being put to the sword, but also with the very real danger of famine and plague sweeping across Connacht, the authorities surrendered on 12 April 1652. Following the siege, Bollingbrook fort fell into disuse as it had served its purpose and was no longer required.

The fort was later strengthened and utilised by French troops defending the town during the Jacobite/Williamite War of 1689–91. However, it fell into enemy hands as all efforts to halt the advance of the Williamite army proved futile. The city came under siege again, this time by the forces of William of Orange, and surrendered after one week. Bollingbrook fort was again vacated and over time it fell into a ruinous state. Nevertheless, it was still described as a 'star-shaped' fort on Bellin's plan of 1764 (Jacques Nicolas Bellin Cartographer Group). The fort is also included on the first edition of the Ordnance Survey map, 1833–42. In the town plan of Galway published in 1872 it is depicted as a fort with linear earthworks to the north-west. The 1893 Ordnance Survey map shows the fort, but the linear earthworks are not shown, indicating that they had disappeared by this time. The *Archaeological Inventory of County Galway* (Volume I, 1993) describes the site as 'the poorly preserved remains of a roughly square earthen artillery fort'. The inventory also suggests that the linear earthworks were 'probably part of the entrenchments connected with the forts'.

In the late seventeenth century this section of land belonged to John Bollingbrook, hence the name. It was referred to as Bollingbrook's Park in the Eyre documents of Galway when Edward Eyre (mayor of Galway) purchased the land, in 1710, from John Bollingbrook, whose address was given as Castlereagh, County Roscommon.

A protection order was placed on the site in August 1977. Part of it was excavated and recorded in 1991 and during the work a small number of artefacts were recovered, including a musket ball, pottery sherds, animal bone and shell fragments. Although the area around the site has been developed in recent times, the remains of the fort have been protected. Bollingbrook fort stands today as a physical reminder of a tragic period in the history of Galway; a time when hardship and terror were part of everyday life.[34]

Tom Hynes and the Great Marathon of the West

During the medieval period in Galway, the main athletic events were held over three days, beginning on 1 May, and were presided over by an appointed Lord and Lady of the May. The mayor and members of the corporation, dressed in all their finery, attended. Houses in the town were decorated with branches of trees and flowers,

---

34   W. Henry, 'Bollingbrook Fort', *St Patrick's Parish Magazine* 1996, pp. 23–5.

and a Maypole was set up in a convenient area of the town, around which people danced in the evenings, while bonfires blazed, adding to the excitement. The games consisted of running, jumping, wrestling and weight-throwing, with much of the activity centring on Eyre Square. On the third day the young men of the town would ride out to Blake's Hill and dine at a location between the Hill and Barna. This signalled the end of the games.[35]

Over time sporting clubs were formed and official events were organised, producing some outstanding sportsmen. The Galway Athletic Club was founded in 1908, and one of its founders was the famous Tom Hynes of Newcastle, who was considered one of Ireland's greatest athletes. Tom came to prominence on St Stephen's Day in 1900 when he won the Connacht Cross Country Championship at Athenry. The following year he won the Irish Junior Cross Country Championships in Dublin. He also won the eighteen-mile professional marathon run between Dublin and Naas in 1904. A year later he finished second in the four-mile scratch race held in Celtic Park in New York. This was followed two weeks later by him winning the five-mile event at the same venue. One of his most distinguished feats was winning the first-ever Irish marathon, held in Dublin in May 1909. Crowds welcomed Hynes home to Galway when he arrived at the railway station and his enthusiastic supporters carried him shoulder-high through the streets of the town. He repeated the same victory the following year. During his

---

35 M. D. O'Sullivan, *Old Galway* (Galway: Facsimile reproduction, Kenny's Bookshop & Art Galleries, 1983), p. 440.

career Tom Hynes won countless championships and held five Irish records, including the five, ten, fifteen, twenty and twenty-six mile championships.[36]

The Galway Athletic Club organised the first marathon race in Connacht for 3 October 1909 as part of a day of athletics held at Eyre Square. The race attracted the highest level of long-distance runners in Ireland. The advertisements in *The Connacht Tribune* requested that people from all over Connacht attend. Entry to Eyre Square on the day was 1s 6d. The event brought record crowds to Galway and special fares were offered by the Midland Great Western Railway Company to ensure a large attendance. Although the main event was advertised as 'The Great Marathon of the West', it was run over fifteen miles and was not the full distance race of today. Nevertheless, it was still a tough race, as the track used was the pathway inside the railings of Eyre Square, which the athletes had to lap continually. The square was thronged with people: men, women and children of all ages gathered for the great event. There was a festive atmosphere all around the town, which continued until the marathon was over. Places in Eyre Square were at a premium as the crowd jostled for a good position. However, as the race progressed, people became more relaxed and many sat down around the track and watched the athletes as they battled for the front position. The local people were in the majority and, of course, cheered and encouraged their own hero, Tom Hynes. As the runners increased their strides during the final laps, the crowd again took to their feet amid cheers and

---

36   'Two Great Galway Athletes', *Galway Advertiser*, 3 August 1986.

great applause. Hynes won the race in 1 hour 27 minutes
and 28 seconds. J. Timmons of Oldcastle took second place
and F. Curtis of Ashbourne came in third. Both these men
were from County Meath. The first prize that day was £10,
with second place receiving £3 and third being awarded
£2. Hynes repeated the victory at the Grammar School on
College Road the following year for the same prize money.
He was described in a local newspaper as the 'best Marathon
runner in Ireland, if not indeed the world'.[37]

Although successful, the Galway Athletic Club was
dissolved in 1914, possibly due to the outbreak of the Great
War, when many of the young men enlisted for service. In
1925 Larry Hynes (son of Tom) revived it for a short time,
but it survived for less than five years. Others involved in
the revival were Paddy Duggan of Newcastle, Jack O'Reilly
of Fairhill, Tom Lally of St Brendan's Avenue and Michael
McDermott from Woodquay.

Galway Victoria Cross Winners

The courage of Irishmen on the field of battle has
never been in doubt. Irish regiments are renowned
for their bravery, with medals for gallantry being awarded
to many. They have fought in wars throughout the world,

---

37   'Western Marathon', *The Connacht Tribune*, 9 October 1909.

even fighting on both sides in various conflicts such as the Mexican–American War, American Civil War, Spanish Civil War and many other struggles. Throughout the eighteenth and nineteenth centuries Ireland became an important recruiting ground for the British army and thousands flocked to its ranks.

The Victoria Cross is the highest military award within the British Empire and is one of the most coveted and prestigious medals for gallantry in the world. It was initiated by Queen Victoria in 1856 and was first awarded for gallantry during the Crimean War of 1853–56.[38] Hancocks & Co., a jewellers on Bruton Street, London, was commissioned to produce the new medal and Queen Victoria took a special interest in its design. The new decoration was made from base metal and the first casting did not impress the Queen. She said that while the cross looked very well in form, she felt the metal was ugly – it was copper and not bronze, and would look very heavy on a red coat. Following these remarks, it was decided to use the bronze from Russian cannons captured in the Crimea for the new medals. The commanding officer of Woolwich Barracks then placed two eighteen-pounder guns at the disposal of the jewellers for the production of the medals. The guns, however, were in fact Chinese and not Russian.

Unlike similar awards, the Victoria Cross is not made in a dye: it is cast in sand moulds usually containing four specimens at a time. The suspender bar, from which the

---

38   R. Doherty and D. Truesdale, *Irish Winners of the Victoria Cross* (Dublin: Four Courts Press, 1993), pp. 12–15.

cross is hung, is cast at the same time as the medal. Once this process is complete, they are removed and finished by skilled craftsmen. It was customary to produce twelve Victoria Crosses at a time. The metal is now held in the army base at Donnington in Telford, Shropshire, and it is estimated that there is only enough remaining to produce eighty more medals.[39]

The Queen selected 26 June 1857 as the presentation day for the first Victoria Cross winners and the ceremony took place during an impressive parade in Hyde Park, London. She attended on horseback and presented the decorations. Since its inception in 1856, the Victoria Cross has been awarded to 166 Irishmen, a figure that represents 12 per cent of the total awarded. Galway is well represented among these figures, producing at least nine Victoria Cross winners.[40] The following is a list of the nine known recipients:

Colour Sergeant Cornelius Coughlan (75th Regiment)

Cornelius Coughlan was born in Eyrecourt on 27 June 1828. He won the VC during action in the Indian Mutiny on 8 June 1857. Upon retiring from the army he returned to Ireland and died in Westport, County Mayo, on 14 February 1915. His VC is in the collection of the Scottish United Services Museum. (No memorial.)[41]

39 'History of the Victoria Cross', www.thevictoriacross.net/history/index. html (accessed June 2009).
40 Doherty and Truesdale, *Irish Winners of the Victoria Cross*, pp. 12–15.
41 *Ibid.*, p. 197.

Private John Doogan (1st King's Dragoon Guards)
John Doogan was born in March 1853 at Aughrim. He was awarded the VC for action at Lang's Nek, South Africa on 28 January 1881. He died in Folkestone, Kent, on 24 January 1940. There is a memorial to him in Shorncliffe Military Cemetery, Kent. Unfortunately, his Victoria Cross was stolen during the 1957 Centenary Exhibition and is now in a private collection in the United States.[42]

Private John Duane (1st Battalion, 60th Battalion or the King's Royal Rifle Corps)
John Duane is also listed as Divane and Devine. He was born in November 1828 at Canavane, Loughrea. Following action on 10 September 1857 during the Indian Mutiny, he was awarded the VC. He displayed extraordinary courage during an attack on enemy positions at Delhi's Kashmir Gate when the city was besieged. John Duane died on 1 December 1888 at New Street, Penzance, Cornwall, and was buried in a pauper's grave. His death notice described him as a 'fish hawker' and army pensioner. In 1995 military historian Ted Lever traced the grave and the Royal Green Jackets erected an appropriate memorial over the site.[43]

Private Thomas Grady (4th or The King's Own Regiment)
Thomas Grady was born on 18 September 1835 at Cheddah (Claddagh). He was awarded the VC at Sebastopol for action that took place between October and November 1854 during the Crimean War. His was the first VC to

---

42   *Ibid.*, p. 200.
43   *Ibid.*, p. 201.

be presented to this regiment. He was also awarded the Distinguished Conduct Medal. Thomas Grady died in Australia on 18 May 1891 and he is remembered on the Australian War Memorial in Canberra. His VC is part of the Australian War Memorial collection.[44]

Private Patrick Green (75th Regiment)
Patrick Green was born in Ballinasloe in 1842. He received his VC for action in the Indian Mutiny on 11 September 1857. Patrick Green died in Cork on 19 July 1889. His medal was sold in May 1926 for £26 to an unknown buyer. (No memorial.)[45]

Gunner Thomas Laughnan (Bengal Artillery)
Thomas Laughnan was born at Kilmacduagh, Gort, in August 1824. He was awarded the VC during the Indian Mutiny on 14 November 1857. He died in County Galway on 23 July 1864. His VC forms part of the Royal Artillery collection. (No memorial.)[46]

Private John Purcell (9th Queen's Royal Lancers)
John Purcell was born at Kilcommon, Oughterard, in 1814. On 19 June 1857 he won the VC for action during the Indian Mutiny. He died at Delhi on 19 September 1857. (No memorial.)[47]

---

44   *Ibid.*, p. 208.
45   *Ibid.*
46   *Ibid.*, pp. 215–216.
47   *Ibid.*, p. 228.

Drummer Dudley Stagpoole (57th Regiment of Foot)

Dudley Stagpoole was born at Killunan, County Galway, in 1838. He was awarded the VC following action in New Zealand on 2 October 1863. He died on 1 August 1911 at Ware, Hertfordshire, in England. There is a memorial to him in Hendon Park Cemetery, London. He was also awarded the Distinguished Conduct Medal. His VC is now part of the Princess of Wales' Royal Regiment collection.[48]

Sergeant Major Alexander Young (Cape Police, South African Forces)

Alexander Young was born on 27 January 1873 at Ballinona, Clarinbridge. He was a brother of the well-known Galway businessman and politician, Joe Young. Alexander Young was educated in the Model School and enlisted in the 2nd Dragoon Guards in 1890 at Renmore Barracks. He was an excellent horseman and became one of the finest rough riders in the British army.[49] He later joined the Royal Scots Greys and became a riding instructor at Canterbury. On 13 August 1901, Young earned the VC during action against several companies of Boers under the command of Commandant Erasmus. The Boers were setting explosives to destroy a railway line, which would prevent Irish troops from reaching their comrades. Young ordered his men to attack and quickly galloped ahead of them. Upon reaching the enemy, he shot several of them and captured their commander. Field Marshal Roberts commended his bravery and Young was presented with his VC by King Edward

48   *Ibid.*, p. 232.
49   *Ibid.*, pp. 99, 234.

VII.[50] He held the rank of lieutenant in the 4th Regiment SA Infantry during the Great War of 1914–1918. He was killed during the Somme offensive on 19 October 1916 and is remembered on the Thiepval Memorial, France.[51]

Lynch's Rock

There is a large rock located in the grounds of the Holy Family School (Woodlands) on the Dublin road near Renmore. How it actually found its way there is not known, but it could possibly be an erratic rock laid down by the ice sheets as they melted some 10,000 years ago. It is known as Lynch's Rock. Some sources indicate that the rock is named after Pyerse (Peter) Lynch, who became the first mayor of Galway in 1485. His brother, Dominick Lynch Fitz-John, more commonly known as Dominick Dubh Lynch, had secured a royal charter from King Richard III, which gave the people of Galway the power to elect a mayor and corporation annually. The brothers also began setting boundaries outside the walled city. Lynch's Rock is exactly one Irish mile from St Nicholas' Collegiate Church, and it seems that one of them named the area 'Milestone', now

---

50   'A Galway V.C.', *The Connacht Tribune*, 9 October 1915.
51   Doherty and Truesdale, *Irish Winners of the Victoria Cross*, pp. 99, 234.

believed to be the smallest townland in Ireland.[52]

In January 1596, during the Nine Years' War, Red Hugh O'Donnell and his army from Ulster set up camp at Lynch's Rock and from there made an attempt to enter the city. O'Donnell was refused supplies and access to the town, so he began burning the eastern suburbs just outside the city walls. He then assembled his forces on Forthill, which was occupied by the Augustinians, and prepared to attack the town. The garrison in the town reacted with cannon fire from the city walls. Meanwhile, an armed party sailed out from the town and landed near the shore at Forthill. Attacking the hill, they soon forced O'Donnell to retreat. His main army was then dislodged from its camp at Lynch's Rock. During his retreat through the county, he burned every village in his path.[53] Incidentally, Red Hugh O'Donnell survived the Nine Years' War and went to Spain, where he died in 1602, having been poisoned by James Blake of Galway.[54]

There is also the possibility that the rock was named after the Lynch family who owned the land and lived in Renmore House close by. A school now occupies this house.

52 N. Sheerin, *Renmore and its Environs: A Historical Perspective: Long Live Yesterday* (Galway: Renmore Residents Association, 2000), p. 50.
53 Hardiman, *History of the Town and County*, pp. 95–7.
54 A. H. Crealey, *An Irish Almanac* (Cork: Mercier Press, 1993), p. 114.

William Henry

The Fishery Field Lime Kiln

This lime kiln is located on the west bank of the River Corrib in the north-west corner of Fishery Field, now in the grounds of the National University of Ireland, Galway. It is rectangular (9.07 metres in length, 6.50 metres in width and 4.20 metres high) and constructed mainly of limestone, but also some sandstone. The puirin, or opening, in the north wall served a dual purpose: setting the fire and retrieving the lime. The south and west walls of the structure each have supporting buttresses.

English settlers introduced lime kilns into Ireland during the seventeenth century and by the eighteenth century a simple but highly effective method of producing lime had developed. Over time this method of lime production spread across Ireland and remained in practice until the 1950s, when powerful limestone crushers replaced it. Because of its large size, the lime kiln in Fishery Field is believed to have been constructed as a commercial enterprise – a factory for supplying lime to businesses and homes around the city. In fact, it is recorded as a factory on the 1833 Ordnance Survey map. There was a house located on top of the kiln until recent times.

Lime kilns are important archaeological monuments as they are a link to an older generation of Irish people whose way of life has now disappeared into the realms of folk history. The location and design of the kiln was crucial. It was important to construct it close to a soft limestone source, and the building materials of the actual kiln needed to be hard limestone or sandstone. Some were built into the sides of hills with the shape of the kiln cut into the earth, thus providing easy access to the structure from above. In areas where no natural hill occurred, such as Fishery Field, a ramp of earth and rock was constructed. The lower section of the structure was erected so that the fire-grate of the furnace was situated about 30 cm off the ground. Although iron was available, it was not used, as it tended to warp in the extreme temperatures of the furnace. Long, narrow stones – similar to stone lintels used over doors and windows – were used instead, and were laid about 2.5 cm apart to act as bars for the grate. At the base of the kiln, a hole about 30 cm square gave access to a tunnel, which was situated directly beneath the furnace. This allowed a steady flow of air into the furnace while allowing for the removal of ash and lime as it fell through the stone lintels above. In most cases, the kiln was plastered with a thick coating of common subsoil called 'Do-Bui' or 'Daub', which acted as a highly efficient insulator.

A good supply of turf and timber was required to produce lime. To ignite the fuel a large bed of highly flammable material was required, and traditionally this consisted of dried vegetation. On top of the flammable bed a heavy layer of turf at least 60 cm thick was laid. The quarried limestone was shattered into small pieces and a layer of this broken limestone, about 30 cm thick, was then placed on top of the turf. Layers of fuel and limestone were laid on top of each other until the kiln was full. Once the furnace was set alight from the bottom, water-soaked sections of earth were placed on top of the kiln, forming the cover. This ensured that maximum heat levels were maintained in the furnace. As the contents of the kiln burned, the tunnel at the base had to be kept clear of ash and lime. In the meantime the cover at the top was removed, using pitchforks. More fuel and limestone were then added in the same order and freshly wetted earth was again utilised to seal in the heat. Attending to a kiln was a twenty-four-hour operation until the required amount of lime was obtained. On average, the whole process could take three or four days, but this obviously depended on the size of the kiln.

The lime produced was used as fertiliser by tillage farmers and spread in gardens locally. This Fishery Field kiln also supplied lime to the nearby Galway jail, workhouse and fever hospital. Lime was also used to whitewash thatched houses and acted as a deterrent to many insects. It could be used in mortar and plaster, and in the production of lime putty. The traditional method of lime production was time-consuming and labour intensive. This led to the acquisition of large limestone quarries by private enterprises. Farmers and other consumers were happy to buy imported lime at a reasonable price when it became available, which signalled the demise of the local lime kilns. They have now gained monument status.

There is another smaller example of a kiln at Tirellan, which was once owned by the Casserly family.

The stone used for the production of lime was extracted from local quarries located at Angliham and on the old road to Coolough and Menlo.[55] The kiln was restored by Galway

---

55   W. Henry, 'Lime Kiln', *Archaeological Survey*, County Galway, 1993, pp. 1–4.

Civic Trust in 2007 and stands as testament to an important chapter in Galway's social history.

Glean Gort an Airgead/ the Duelling Field

*G*lean Gort an Airgead (Field in the Glen of Money) is a large, open field located adjacent to the old Dublin road in Roscam. According to folklore, this stretch of road was a favourite haunt of highwaymen during the eighteenth and early nineteenth centuries. It was an excellent choice for these 'stand and deliver' men, as coaches on the way into Galway had to slow down because of the hill. A natural canopy of trees also covered this section of road and the dark, wooded area on either side provided excellent cover for the bandits. The coaches proved easy targets as they laboured up the old dirt road.

According to local tradition, some highwaymen hid their 'loot' in this locality and would retrieve it at a later stage, hence the name *Glean Gort an Airgead*. There were two notorious Galway characters who plied their trade in this area. They were eventually captured and were tried for highway robbery at Galway Court House. By the 1830s there were still many offences punishable by death, but it seems that many jurors were merciful. The highwaymen found themselves standing before Judge Fletcher, who by all accounts seems to have been a bit of a character himself. There was a weight of damning evidence against the defendants, and knowing the penalty attached to a guilty verdict, the prisoners were worried. However, when the jury returned, having deliberated for some time, they astonished the court as well as the prisoners by finding them not guilty. The judge knew that before him were two very guilty highwaymen, but there was nothing he could do about it now that the jury had passed its verdict. To let all present know that he had not been fooled by the proceedings, he addressed the jailer just as the defendants were being removed from the dock, saying: 'Mr Walsh, you will greatly ease my mind if you would keep those respectable gentlemen until seven o'clock, or half-past seven, for I mean to set out for the Ennis Assizes at five, and I should like to have two hours' start of them.'[56]

This field is also known by two other names: the Field of Mars or, more commonly, the Duelling Field. From the late seventeenth to the about the mid-nineteenth century duelling was a highly respected method of gun and sword fighting, and was a way for many gentlemen to settle disputes. Duelling was practised throughout Ireland, but Galway and Tipperary were two of the main counties where gentlemen became supreme exponents of the art and settled many quarrels from behind the barrel of a pistol or at the point of a sword.[57] One gunfight that took place in the Duelling Field

---

56 S. McGuire, 'Law and Order in Galway', *Galway Reader*, vol. 4, nos 2, 3, 1954, p. 63.

57 W. Henry, *St Clerans: The Tale of a Manor House* (Galway: Merv Griffin, 1999), p. 15.

was recorded by Sir William Gregory in his autobiography, published in 1894. The following is his account of the duel, which was witnessed by a local man he met while on his way to Galway in 1841:

> The first year [1841] that I came to Coole, I rode one day into Galway. When I got to Merlin Park, I asked a countryman the name of the place, and found him, as one always finds Irish peasants, most agreeable and communicative. 'I suppose you know all about that field,' he said pointing to the one opposite the wall of Merlin Park.
>
> 'No,' said I, 'I'm quite a stranger.'
>
> 'Well sir,' he said, 'that's the place where the gentlemen of Galway used to fight their duels. Many's the duel I saw there when I was young, for I live quite convenient.'
>
> 'Did you ever see a real good duel?' I asked.
>
> 'To be sure I did, and lots of them. But the best I ever saw was between Councillor Browne and Dr Bodkin, I have forgotten their real names. It was a beautiful morning, with a fine bright sun. Young Lynch, the attorney's son of Oranmore, was Councillor Browne's second, and won the toss. So he put the councillor with his back to the sun, and the doctor's second never saw what was going to happen till it was too late. The poor doctor came up winking and blinking, and at the very first offer the councillor shot him dead. It was a grand shot, your honour. The doctor sprang up three feet in the air, and fell on his face and never spoke another word. Faith! Young Lynch was a grand second that day!'[58]

Richard Martin was one of the most famous duellists of the period and was an expert with both pistols and swords. He is reputed to have fought over 100 duels during his lifetime, many of them, it seems, in the Duelling Field. It was his reputation as a gunman that earned him the nickname

58   Sheerin, *Renmore and its Environs*, p. 87.

'Hair-Trigger Dick'. One legendary duel in which Martin took part involved a celebrated continental duellist. This gentleman often wore a suit of light but strong chainmail beneath his clothing. Of course, this was totally against the rules, but he managed to conceal his protection on most occasions. On the morning that he faced Martin, he fitted his body armour and set out for the field. However, one of Richard Martin's servants discovered the secret and rushed to Martin's side, saying to him, in Irish so the continental man would not understand, *'Buial e mar mharbhuigheann fear Conaqmara an mhuc,'* meaning 'Hit him where the Connemara man kills the pig.' Martin, also known as the 'King of Connemara', knew exactly what he had to do. He took quick but careful aim and shot his opponent in the side of the head, killing him instantly. (Some sources attribute this story to a different duel.)

Martin's reputation with a duelling pistol often helped diffuse difficult situations. On one occasion during a dinner party at his home an argument broke out between the guests. Turning to a servant close by, he said in a loud voice, 'Melt the lead, John.' His remark had the desired effect and cooled the situation immediately.[59] Richard Martin was also known as 'Humanity Martin' because of his kindness towards animals. He was the first man to have laws passed to protect them.

The old Dublin road still has a canopy of trees and many people drive by this tranquil field today without realising its violent past.

---

59   M. Barry, *An Affair of Honour* (Fermoy: Eigse, 1981), pp. 124–5.

Roscam Folly

A folly is an ornamental structure constructed mainly for decoration and with no useful or practical purpose, although its appearance may well suggest otherwise. Follies could be costly to construct, both in labour and materials. During the eighteenth and early nineteenth centuries it became fashionable, and somewhat of a status symbol, for landlords to have an ancient monument located on their land. Where none existed, some landlords had a 'monument' erected to embellish their estates, built primarily to be viewed as part of the scenery.

Following the discovery of Pompeii and other classical sites, travellers embarked on exotic expeditions to places such as Ephesus, Troy, Antioch and Rhodes, from where many took their inspiration for their folly designs. At their height, these locations also attracted poets and artists who endeavoured to capture and preserve the spirit and melancholy beauty of such places. Follies were erected in various classical designs. There were also finely decorated stone archways that would lead 'nowhere'. Some structures looked like miniature Greek or Roman temples; others were similar to church sites. Extreme examples were simply 'conversation pieces' as they had no function at all and were an invention of the builder's imagination. People were simply left to ponder and speculate as to their purpose.[60]

---

60   W. Henry, 'Tour of Roscam', Tour Leaflet, Galway, 1995.

The Roscam folly could fall into this category. The landowners in this area were the Davenport family and it is believed that they had the folly – a circular stone structure that rises in tiers, growing smaller towards the top – erected sometime during the nineteenth century. A number of theories have been put forward regarding its purpose. Some people say it resembles an Aztec sacrificial shrine, while others say it supported some type of lookout post. It has also been suggested that it was designed for loading certain types of carts or wagons, or that it was a type of lighthouse: a fire could be lit on the top, as Galway Bay is close by. A very finely built cut-stone wall containing recesses that were probably designed to hold beehives surrounds the structure. However, like most other follies the Roscam example was probably purely a decoration and acted as a centrepiece for the walled garden on the Davenport estate.[61]

The Bodkin Murders

There was a time when crime was dealt with quickly and severely, and many towns and cities had their own gallows, flogging posts and stocks. Galway was no exception: the famous 1651 pictorial map of the town bears

---

61   E. Fox, M. Leonard and P. O'Dowd, *Introduction to Burrenology* (Galway: Regional Technical College, 1978), p. 50.

testament to a gallows, complete with victim. The gallows stood approximately halfway between the Browne Doorway and the Bank of Ireland at 43 Eyre Square. Many victims were left to hang there for long periods as a warning to other would-be criminals, and this must have been a sobering sight upon entering the old city. Another gallows was situated opposite the New Cemetery at Bohermore and a nearby road once bore the name the 'Auld Gallows'.

There was very little time for appeals against sentences in those days – the period between arrest, trial and execution of sentence could be less than a week. However, while the gallows at Eyre Square was in regular use, its victims are not widely known, with the exception of John Bodkin, a descendant of the famous tribal family of Galway. His path to the gallows began at Carrowbeg House near Tuam, where the infamous 'Bodkin Murders' were planned. The shocking crimes themselves took place at Carrowbawn House, about four miles from Tuam on the road towards Headford.

Sometime around 1720 Oliver Bodkin married and his first son, John, was born shortly afterwards.[62] (For the purpose of this section and to avoid confusion, his son will henceforth be referred to as 'young John'.) Oliver and his wife showered the child with love and affection to a degree that he was spoiled beyond reason. Oliver Bodkin's wife died in 1730, leaving him with the responsibility of rearing the young child. Bodkin later married Margery Blake of Oranmore and also had a son with his second wife, whom

---

62   J. O'Connell, 'The Bodkin Murders', *Galway Reader*, vol. 4, no. 1, 1953, pp. 123–4.

he named Oliver. It was customary for some families at this time to have a new baby cared for by an employee of the house, and later returned to the natural parents. Baby Oliver was given over to John Hogan and his wife, who were tenants of the Bodkins. The child displayed much affection towards his adoptive family: in fact, he called Hogan 'Daddy'. When he was three years old, Oliver was returned to his family. His father displayed as much affection towards Oliver as he had towards his first child, and young John became extremely jealous of his half-brother.[63]

Young John was later sent to Trinity College in Dublin. He was not overly interested in the path chosen for him, and seems to have enjoyed his new surroundings to such a degree that he neglected his studies. Because of this he was forced to leave Trinity and return to Carrowbawn House. His father and stepmother frowned upon his behaviour in Trinity. Young John's stepmother also saw him as a threat to her own son's inheritance. Young John resented her attitude and over a relatively short time developed an intense hatred for his stepmother, while his jealousy of his half-brother deepened. His feelings overwhelmed him so much that he left Carrowbawn House in 1737.

Young John was about seventeen years old at the time and went to stay with his uncle, also named John Bodkin, at Carrowbeg House, situated about a mile west of Carrowbawn House. John Bodkin had two sons, John and Patrick, and it seems that he spent much of his time away from home as he

---

63   T. Claffey, 'The Bodkin Murders', lecture to the Old Galway Society, 10 October 1996.

was a barrister and often worked in Dublin. In his absence his brother, Dominick Bodkin, who was known as Blind Dominick because he was blind in one eye, looked after the property. He had a distorted, pock-marked face, the result of childhood smallpox. Blind Dominick was unmarried and had no inheritance to look forward to in old age. (Some sources indicate that young John was already spending time in the company of Blind Dominick before he went to Trinity and that upon returning he went directly to live at Carrowbeg House.[64]) Blind Dominick had a dreadful reputation with the local people and was not trusted or liked by them. Young John confided his grievances about his father and stepmother to this uncle.

A short time later young John's cousin Patrick was found dead in bed one morning. At the time, no one paid particular attention to his death, believing that eating a large feed of salty bacon late the previous night had caused it, so no real investigation took place.

In the spring of 1741 young John learned that his father had altered his will, leaving his entire estate to his second son, Oliver. Oliver Bodkin also confided to a friend, a justice of the peace from Athenry, that he felt that his eldest son, young John, was going to do some 'mischief' to him. Young John was furious and in a fit of rage decided that his only option to secure what he felt was his rightful inheritance was to murder his family. When he mentioned his gruesome plan to his uncle, Blind Dominick, he immediately found a willing accomplice. They enlisted the help of John Hogan,

---

64   O'Connell, 'Bodkin Murders', pp. 124–5.

who had acted as a guardian to young Oliver.[65] On the night of Friday 18 September 1741, the conspirators met at Carrowbeg House and set about planning the murders. They had included the barrister's son John in the plotting, but he became nervous and left the house not wanting any involvement. Nevertheless, the others began making their brutal plans over a bottle of whiskey. It was the week of the Galway Races, usually held near Loughrea at that time, but the date and venue had been changed to accommodate some of the legal fraternity and landed gentry. The races were to be held that particular week in Tuam. Young John announced that he would go to the races while the others carried out the murders. He felt this would take suspicion away from him, but the other two conspirators would not agree, telling him that if he wished to see his family dead then he would have to play his part in the murders. Before departing, Blind Dominick produced two long knives, which he said he would sharpen. The following night the killers met outside Carrowbawn House and made their way into the grounds, where they began to put their vicious plan into action.

The first victims on that dreadful night were two sheepdogs. Both dogs knew the killers and did not bark, but rather approached them expecting to be stroked. Instead, they had their throats cut. The three murderers then went in silence to the servants' quarters, where they found two workmen and two servant boys. All four had their throats cut also. Upon entering the main section of the house, they came across another workman and his wife, both of

---

65   *Ibid.*, pp. 125–6.

whom they stabbed through the heart. The next victim was a Galway merchant named Marcus Lynch, a friend of the family who happened to be staying at the house that night as he had been attending the races. John Hogan then made his way to the main bedroom where he cut the throats of Oliver Bodkin and his wife. So brutal was the attack that he almost decapitated them.[66] He then turned his attention to little seven-year-old Oliver, who was sleeping in the same room. As Hogan approached the bed the child, who was already awake, cried out, 'Daddy, Daddy, don't kill me!' Hogan must have felt some degree of pity because rather than kill the child he smeared him with blood and made him lie still, hoping that the others would think he was dead.

However, Blind Dominick sensed what was happening and forced Hogan to kill the boy. Hogan used so much force that he decapitated the child in the process.[67] His head was then placed on the body of his murdered father.

There is another version of how Margery Bodkin, who was heavily pregnant at the time, died. In this, Hogan and her stepson let her out of the room. She ran down the stairs and was making her way through the kitchen when Blind Dominick caught her and stabbed her a number of times, killing both her and her unborn baby.

Thus eleven people were murdered in the most frightening and shocking manner on that night of horror.

The following day a horrified crowed gathered outside the house where the ghastly deeds had taken place. News

66   Claffey, 'Bodkin Murders'.
67   O'Connell, 'Bodkin Murders', pp. 126–7.

was spreading of the gruesome scene that lay just beyond the threshold of the house and was now being investigated by the police. Among the crowd was one of the murderers, young John, trying to feign anguish at the death of his father and step-family. However, some of the people noticed that there were bloodstains on his clothing. This caused immediate suspicion and he was arrested and taken to Galway jail. Once in custody he made a full confession, implicating his two accomplices.

On 6 October 1741 the three murderers were brought under military escort to Tuam for trial. They were held overnight and the trial, the following day, took fourteen hours. The jury, however, only took ten minutes to reach a guilty verdict. The trio received the sentence of death. It was to be swift justice: they were sentenced to be hanged on the following day. It was customary at that time to hang murderers as close as possible to the location where they committed the crime, thus the three murderers were brought by cart to Clare-Tuam, a place close to the murder scene, where they were hanged from a tree. Following the hanging, Hogan's head was hacked off and taken back to Tuam where it was placed on a spike on top of the market-house. The bodies of the other murderers were dismembered and their body parts placed on stakes at various locations along the road to Tuam to act as a warning and to show that justice had been served. It was said that people would not sow crops near any of these gruesome sights for fear of contamination. The remains of the murderers were later collected and buried in an unmarked grave near to where the murders had taken place.

Before young John was hanged, he requested permission to make a statement. During his testimony he referred to the earlier death of his cousin, Patrick Bodkin, at Carrowbeg House. He said that Patrick's younger brother John, in a bid to take all of his father's inheritance, had murdered Patrick. John, he asserted, had placed a pillow over his brother's face and sat on it until his victim had suffocated. This same John Bodkin was actually attending the executions and heard his cousin's accusations from the gallows. He immediately mounted his horse and escaped, but was eventually captured near Belclare on 22 October 1741 and imprisoned in Galway jail until the following March, when he stood trial for the murder of his brother. Given the swiftness of the other case, it is not clear why so much time elapsed between his arrest and trial, which, on 8 March 1742, took eleven hours. He was found guilty and sentenced to death. The following morning he was taken directly to Eyre Square, known locally at the time as 'Gallows Green'. He was asked to admit to his crime but would not comment either way. Bodkin was then hanged and decapitated. His head was taken to Tuam to be placed in a cage on public display.

Carrowbawn House was demolished in a bid to wipe out the memory of the killings, which must rank as one of the most horrific crimes ever committed in the history of this country.[68]

---

68   Claffey, 'Bodkin Murders'.

The Renmore Races

One could not live in Galway without knowing of the Galway Races, which have taken place at Ballybrit annually since 1869. Many people would also remember, or at least have heard of, horse racing taking place in The Swamp (now called South Park) near the Claddagh. However, very few people are aware that horse racing also took place in Renmore. Billed as the 'first annual Renmore Races', this meeting took place on Monday 10 June 1957. Crowds arrived from all over the county to attend the races, which were actually located in Fahy's Field. The uncertain weather conditions did not deter people. There were six races in all: The Mervue Plate, an open pony race for registered Connemara ponies, was won by Dancing Spanner; The Oranmore Stakes, an open race, was won by Red Rocket; The Corrib Plate, a pony and cob race, was won by Story of Tina; The Merlin Stakes, another open race, was won by Won't Go; and The Ballybane Stakes was won by Clare Man. The main event of the day was the Renmore Plate, which was run over two miles. The winner was a horse called No Surprise, and this was no surprise to almost everyone attending, as he was the favourite.

The races held all the glamour of a typical flapper meeting with a large, excited crowd overwhelming the bookies. There were colourful sideshows, stalls and travelling performers to entertain the crowds. The Galway Pipers' Band (Guth na nÓg Pipers' Band) played for the punters between each race.

One of the outstanding pipers of the day was Francis Hogan of Shantalla, who held the attention of all present. Although the meet was a huge success and showed great promise for the future, it is now consigned to hidden history.[69]

A Christmas Morning Tragedy

Christmas is a time of happiness for most people. However, for some it is a time of tragedy. One of the worst disasters to occur in Ireland during the festive season happened on Christmas morning 1842 when people from around the city, and some indeed from the county, converged on the pro-cathedral (the parish church of St Nicholas, located on the corner of Abbeygate Street Lower and Middle Street) for 6 a.m. mass. It was an inky, dark morning. People greeted each other with Christmas wishes; children skipped along, happy in the knowledge that it was a special morning and that there would be some treats for them later. It had been a bad year overall, with food shortages and even riots in the town, but the worst of the problems had subsided and the New Year, it was hoped, would bring better days. It was also an extraordinarily mild winter, which added to the optimism of the people.

---

69   'Colourful Scenes at Renmore Races', *The Connacht Tribune*, 15 June 1957.

To secure seats, people were gathering in the church for over an hour before mass began. Many were looking forward to the singing. In fact one man, a non-Catholic from Annaghdown, arrived by boat just to experience the sound of the congregation as they sang hymns.

The parish priest was Rev. B. J. Roche. Just as he began to celebrate mass, someone in the gallery shouted that the floor was collapsing – a noise had been heard that sounded like timber splintering. These alarming words instantly spread panic through the congregation and there was a frantic rush to the exits. Some of those trapped in the gallery were so terrified that they threw open the windows and jumped to their deaths in the street below. Others flung themselves over the handrail of the gallery inside the church, killing or injuring themselves and those upon whom they fell. Most of the people, however, tried to get out through the main exit, thus jamming the porch area and making it almost impossible to escape. It was a pitiful scene; the terror and screams of people being crushed in the confined space was appalling. The panic-stricken people, many of them parents with children, tried frantically to reach the safety of the street, which was only a few feet away. An eyewitness recorded: 'for a few moments a scene was witnessed so horrific that it completely baffles description'.[70] Some people did remain calm, among them Fr Roche, who made his way to the altar to call for an end to the panic, while Br Paul O'Connor of the Monastery School forcibly reached the main door and

---

70   'A Christmas Morning Tragedy', *Brat Muire/ The Mantle*, no. 28, 1964, pp. 12–15.

tried to restore order. When the survivors finally reached the safety of the street there was a gloomy silence as they soon realised that the frightful panic was groundless. There had been no danger.

It was a heart-rending scene: thirty-seven people had been killed. Those who were able went to the aid of the injured. Some twenty people were seriously injured and were eventually removed, and those with mild injuries were taken into the Mechanics Institute next door and some to the local barracks and dispensary. As dawn was breaking news of the calamity quickly spread through the town and through the gloom of that Christmas morning people hurried to the scene, enquiring about their relatives. The police and military also arrived to help deal with the pathetic situation. Once the injured were removed, the bodies of those who had lost their lives were placed under flickering gas-lamps along the street for identification.

The inquest began on St Stephen's Day before the coroner, John Blakeney, and a jury of sixteen people. However, it was adjourned until Friday 30 December. There were twenty-four witnesses called to give evidence, including Harry Clare, a stonemason from Forster Street. He was in a room located over the sacristy when the tragedy occurred. During the interview, Clare said that he had heard someone shout from the gallery that the chapel was on fire, but upon investigation he discovered that all was quiet and orderly. Some two or three minutes later he had heard another shout – this time someone called out that the gallery was falling. He also stated that he had heard the sound of splintering timber. The inquest was relatively short and the verdict unanimous:

> We find that the deaths of thirty-seven persons which took place at the Parish chapel of St Nicholas in the County of the Town of Galway, on Christmas morning last, was caused by a rush of the congregation to gain egress, on a cry being groundlessly raised, by some person or persons to us unknown, that the galleries were falling, and that the said alarm was created without any malicious intent.

Fr Roche endorsed the verdict while he was celebrating mass on New Year's Day 1843.

The sad reality, of course, was that there was no real danger. The sound that had caused the panic, resulting in the disaster, was a small fracture in a section of the timber handrail and was of no real consequence. In the days following the tragedy, heartbreaking scenes were witnessed in Galway as the funerals of the victims, many of them children, took place. Seventeen of the victims were buried in one day in Forthill Cemetery. A benevolent fund was subsequently started to help the bereaved families. It was later reported that about 170 people, mainly orphans and elderly, were reduced to poverty because of the tragedy.

It is interesting to note that exactly two years earlier, in 1840, a similar panic occurred at 6 a.m. mass in the Church of St Nicholas of Myra in Francis Street, Dublin. The alarm was also caused by the sound of splintering timber. Three people lost their lives and several others were injured.[71]

---

71   *Ibid.*

John Bodkin's Hand

In around 1320 construction work began on the Church of St Nicholas of Myra in Galway, the burial place for many of the region's celebrated tribal families. At the time, Galway was under the jurisdiction of the archbishopric of Tuam. In 1484 Pope Innocent VIII conferred collegiate status on the church, which meant that the citizens would be governed by a warden and eight vicars rather than a bishop. The church was Roman Catholic until the Protestant Reformation of the sixteenth century and changed hands a number of times during the religious wars of the seventeenth century.[72] In 1690 a man named John Bodkin became the last Catholic warden of St Nicholas' Collegiate Church during the Jacobite–Williamite War, a conflict between the Catholic King James II of England, Ireland and Scotland, and the Protestant William of Orange, who had deposed James in 1688.

A disaster for the Irish Catholics at the Battle of Aughrim in July 1691 dashed any hope of securing the throne for James II. One week later Galway came under siege from a 14,000-strong Williamite army under the command of Godert de Ginkell. Bloody skirmishing took place just outside the city walls, during which Terryland Castle was burned. However, Galway was not prepared for another

---

72   Henry, *Role of Honour*, pp. 22–3.

long siege, such as it had suffered with the Cromwellians some forty years earlier, so articles were agreed and signed on 21 July, and the town surrendered on 26 July.[73]

The surrender also marked the end of Catholic control of St Nicholas' Church. Warden John Bodkin was compelled to hand over the keys to the new Protestant establishment. Some said that the keys had to be forcibly taken from him, and according to tradition Bodkin uttered the following prayer: 'My God, that my right hand may not decay until the keys of this church be restored to the proper owners.'

John Bodkin died in 1710 and his remains were entombed in a vault beneath the church. His prayer regarding the keys was not forgotten and as the Penal Laws eased Catholics began visiting his tomb as a place of pilgrimage. It seems that in the years following his burial, the body of John Bodkin remained in a state of preservation within the tomb and his coffin had to be replaced on three occasions. In the late 1730s some covering flagstones collapsed into the vault, damaging part of his coffin and remains. It was known that some visitors to the church were in fact bribing the sexton (caretaker) to gain entry to the vault to view the body of Bodkin. It was believed that access was gained through a secret underground passage, the entrance to which was located in the floor close to the high altar. There was also supposed to be an entrance to the vault from the cemetery outside the church. In 1813 the body of Warden Bodkin was examined by a sexton of the church named Mr Read, who recorded his findings and confirmed the preservation

---

73   *Ibid.*, p. 93.

of the body. However, he placed the documents inside the coffin with the body and the burial vault was sealed again.

In March 1838 the body of John Bodkin was again disturbed when what was termed a 'remarkable discovery' was made by workmen carrying out repairs on the vaults and tombs near the main altar of the church. The workmen were under the supervision of Henry Clare from Forster Street. While work was in progress, people began frequenting the church. Many of them pointed out to the workmen the location of the vault (the entrance was recorded at the time as being to the right of the high altar) and informed them of the story of John Bodkin's prayer and how his body had not decayed. Eventually, Clare decided to open the vault and later recorded:

> … upon opening the vault I was the first to descend. I found the body of a man, all perfect, except for his toes. Many of the by-standers stated that they had been broken off by one of the covering flags that broke and fell into the vault 100 years before this date. The hands were in all appearance perfect, even to the nails and fingers, not discoloured. The face perfect, the ears and top of the nose, all the teeth were perfectly white, all the skin [not] discoloured. By pressing my hand on any part of this body, it felt quite elastic.

Once news of the discovery reached the streets there was huge excitement and interest among the population of the town and many came to view the remains. Rumours spread throughout the city and county that old Bodkin still held the keys firmly in his hand, which of course was false. Speculation and talk about supernatural phenomena regarding the preservation of the body drew thousands to the church. Local people were mystified by the events unfolding in their community. They witnessed many people, including descendents of the old families of Galway, forcing their way into the church to try to gain access to the vault. Chaos ensued and work ceased as the crowds became so dense that it was impossible to continue renovations. By the end of the third day, the church was cleared of people and locked, denying access to the public. Henry Clare gave the keys to the then sexton, Henry Caddy. Both men knew that something would have to be done fast if work was to continue.

Early the following morning, a very agitated foreman carpenter, John McMahon, who had been working in the church, arrived at the home of Henry Clare. He reported that during the night the tomb of old Bodkin had been entered by a person or persons unknown and that the right hand of the warden had been cut off and removed from the church. He also announced that he did not wish to remain in the church for fear he would be blamed: after all, he was a Presbyterian and people might assume that he was responsible. However, there was no need for his anxiety, as suspicion immediately fell upon the sexton, Henry Caddy. When questioned, he insisted that he had had no part in the removal of John Bodkin's hand and denied any knowledge of the crime. His denial was taken by some people as a refusal to cooperate and they threatened to throw Caddy off the nearby West Bridge (later O'Brien's Bridge) into the River Corrib.

The threat seems to have had the desired effect, as Caddy then admitted that he had given the keys of the church to the town commissioner, Timothy Murray, and a local doctor named McSweeney. However, he insisted that he had not taken any part in the removal of the hand. Upon further interrogation, Caddy informed his questioners that a 'party of gentlemen had poured lime and sulphuric acid upon the body but that this action had only discoloured the remains'. As the morning wore on, news of the violation of the corpse and the missing hand incensed the crowd gathering around the church. By midday, there was a growing fear of 'mob violence', and Henry Clare realised that he would have to try to pacify the crowd. He persuaded the people to allow him time to secure the return of the warden's hand and then made his way to the home of Doctor McSweeney.

When confronted by the allegations, McSweeney completely denied possessing the hand. However, when warned of the danger now brewing in the town, he admitted that it had been placed in a pawn shop owned by Timothy Murray and insisted that it was put there for 'safe-keeping'. Clare then enlisted the help of the local parish priest, Fr Roche, in addressing the crowd, which had not dispersed. Fr Roche and Clare promised them that they were investigating the incident and would have the hand returned by the afternoon. The people, once guaranteed that the stolen hand would be returned by 2 p.m. that day, were satisfied. They then dispersed slowly and returned to their homes. They returned at the appointed time and again gathered around St Nicholas' church, but had to wait anxiously for an additional two hours before Henry Clare and Fr Roche arrived. By now thousands of curious spectators had gathered in the narrow streets to see the two men return, as promised, with a parcel containing the old warden's hand.

However, the hand had been subjected to mutilation. The fingers had been cut off and the palm split into pieces as far as the wrist. This angered the crowd. To appease the people John McMahon, the carpenter, already had a new coffin prepared for John Bodkin and his hand. The mutilated hand was then re-united with the corpse and the old warden was once again replaced in the vault.

It was suggested the following day that the remains of Warden Bodkin should be buried in a Catholic cemetery. The Bishop of Galway, George Joseph Browne, referred the case to the Vicar-General, Rev. Laurence O'Donnell. After some deliberation, he decided that it was more appropriate for the body of John Bodkin to remain in the vault of St Nicholas' Church. A short time later the vault was again sealed, and this time the tomb was left unmarked.

It is not known why the hand was mutilated. Was it an attempt to have Bodkin's prayer discredited before the Catholic community, who had only recently gained Emancipation? There is also the possibility that the mutilation was for financial gain – had the perpetrators intended to sell the body parts as souvenirs or relics? Whoever carried out the deed certainly had no fear of supernatural happenings. The story still carries an atmosphere of mystery and as one wanders around this old church in the very heart of Galway one cannot help but wonder about the old warden buried beneath the flagstones.[74]

---

74   C. Riordan, 'Legends of St Nicholas Church Galway: The Mystery of Warden Bodkin's Hand', www.legendquest.ie (May 2010)

The Dead

This is the story of the love affair between Michael Bodkin and young Nora Barnacle, and a tragic twist of fate that changed the course of history for one of Ireland's greatest writers. Nora Barnacle was the lover, and later wife, of the celebrated literary giant James Joyce, but it was her love for Michael Bodkin that inspired Joyce to write his famous short story 'The Dead'.

Nora Barnacle was born in March 1884 in the maternity ward of Galway Workhouse. She was the second child in a family of eight, born to Thomas and Annie Barnacle. Her father was a baker and her mother earned a living as a dressmaker. The family lived in several different areas in Galway city until they finally settled in Bowling Green. As a child, Nora lived for a number of years with her grandmother, Catherine Healy, and her uncle, Thomas, in St Augustine Street. She attended the Convent of Mercy National School until she was twelve. Following the death of her grandmother in 1897, she was looked after by her uncle. Nora's father drank heavily, which resulted in many problems for the family. Her mother eventually forced him to leave the family home. By this time, Nora was a high-spirited, good-looking teenage girl with auburn-coloured hair. She was very popular and had many friends around the town. However, her uncle was very strict and curtailed her movements. Nora secured employment in the Presentation

Convent, which gave her some degree of independence.[75]

During this time, she met and fell in love with seventeen-year-old Michael Bodkin, a student at University College Galway. He worked in Galway Gashouse, presumably to pay his college fees. The Bodkin family owned a shop at 2 Prospect Hill, where Michael also worked when not attending college or working in the Gashouse. His father was Patrick Bodkin from Bushypark, just west of Galway city, and his mother was Winifred Pathe from Cork. They had one other son, Leo. Michael was described as a handsome, pleasant, warm-hearted young man with black wavy hair. There is no record of young Bodkin having graduated from university and it is presumed that he abandoned his studies.

It seems that Nora was attracted by his gentle yet manly manner. This was a time when young lovers had to be careful, and while opportunities to spend time together did not readily present themselves, Nora and Michael managed rather well. Nora would frequent the shop, where they chatted and joked between young Bodkin serving customers. It was rumoured that this was how they met: Nora, sometimes in the company of a friend, sometimes alone, arrived in the shop and passed small pleasantries. While Michael was engaged serving real customers, Nora was busy indulging herself in her favourite sweets. Michael was well aware of Nora and her little routine, but turned a blind eye, as he was falling in love with her.

They eventually began dating and would take the tram to Salthill, a holiday resort some three miles west of the city.

---

75 P. O'Laoi, *Nora Barnacle Joyce: A Portrait* (Galway: Kenny's Bookshops, 1982), pp. 10–11.

There, lost among visiting strangers, they would stroll hand in hand along the shoreline. Having attended Sunday mass they would meet and go for a walk out along the Dyke road as far as the old ruined de Burgo castle at Terryland. They often chased each other through the castle field until they reached the old ruin, then sat in the afternoon sunshine blissfully unaware of the world. From this vantage point they could watch the Galway–Clifden train as it steamed across the great metal bridge that spanned the River Corrib at Woodquay. The train ran by them on the opposite side of the river, making its way towards Connemara, shooting great puffs of white smoke into the air to greet the sky.

Michael was almost three years older than Nora and when he was eighteen he presented her with a bracelet as a token of his love for her. She had just turned sixteen. While it was of little monetary value, it was of immense value to Nora, and she treasured it all her life. Receiving such a gift was significant to her and she believed it was sign of their future together.

Everything seemed so wonderful and natural, the way it should always be for young lovers, but alas, just as their love blossomed into maturity, Michael developed tuberculosis. He was ill for a time and by Christmas 1899 his health had deteriorated greatly. Michael was admitted to the County Infirmary, just a short distance from his home in Prospect Hill. He did not recover and died on 11 February 1900. He was just twenty years old when he was interred in a tomb in Rahoon Cemetery.

Nora was devastated by his death and lost interest in everything. She pined and withdrew from life, and while in this state of grief she confided in a young curate. She would call to the presbytery and talk over her feelings about Michael with him. One evening, while they were having tea, he asked her to sit on his lap. Nora was obviously gullible, as she did as he requested. Moments later his hand began moving up under her dress. She quickly realised what was happening and broke away from him, thus ending her visits to the presbytery.

By 1904 she had met another young man, Willie Mulvagh, and dated him for a time. While he was very much in love with her, she later admitted that she never really loved him. Because he was Protestant, her Catholic family objected to the relationship. Her uncle even resorted to thrashing her with a walking stick. This harsh treatment only added to her desire to leave Galway. According to one story, her father was not in favour of her wanting to go to Dublin, and in a bid to stop her he burned her suitcase full of clothes outside the house on Bowling Green. Nora ran to her friend Katie Hoare's house in Suckeen, borrowed a coat and dress and took the train to Dublin.[76]

Nora secured employment at Finn's Hotel in Leinster Street, just off Nassau Street. She liked hotel work as it gave her the free time to explore her new surroundings. On 10 June 1904, while walking down Nassau Street, she encountered a young man who stood in front of her and struck up a conversation. She was a little taken aback at first by this stranger, wearing a sailor's cap and canvas shoes. However, she saw in him some of Michael Bodkin's features, and as she gazed into his deep blue eyes she became more

---

76   *Ibid.*, pp. 24–5, 37.

comfortable with him. They spoke for a time and arranged to meet each other again on 14 June, but Nora failed to show up for this date. James Joyce wrote a note to her requesting that they meet, this time on 16 June. She turned up on this occasion, and that evening they walked down by the River Liffey towards Ringsend, a walk which changed both of their lives forever. Joyce was very open with Nora and told her of his past escapades and sexual encounters. He was also interested in her past and in particular her romances. He developed a deep love for Nora and liked to hear her singing. Sometimes she would sing the 'Lass of Aughrim', the lyrics of which are based on young woman who, after being seduced and made pregnant by an aristocratic lover, is abandoned by him.[77]

Over time she told him of Michael Bodkin. The story affected Joyce to such a degree that he immortalised their love in his story 'The Dead', which was published in 1907. However, he changed Michael Bodkin's name to Michael Furey, Nora becoming Gretta Conroy, and Bodkin's tomb he records as being in Oughterard Cemetery. In the story, Joyce places his heroine as living in Nun's Island with her grandmother. It was here that a very ill Michael Furey came to see Gretta before she left for Dublin, where she was going to remain until summer. It was a cold, wet night when he arrived in the back garden of the house and threw gravel up at her window. She crept down to meet him and implored him to go home before he caught 'his death' out in such rain. They exchanged words of love and having said their goodbyes

---

77   *Ibid.*, pp. 34–5, 41.

he returned home, where he died a week later. Joyce also used the song 'Lass of Aughrim' in his story. He also referred to Michael Bodkin in his notes on his play *Exiles*.

Joyce and Nora had two children, Giorgio and Lucia, and in July 1912 they all went to Galway to visit Nora's family. While in Galway, they attended the races, visited the Aran Islands and spent some time boating on the River Corrib.[78] It was during this time that they visited Michael Bodkin's tomb in Rahoon Cemetery. Shortly afterwards Joyce wrote a poem, 'She Weeps Over Rahoon', in which he attempted to capture Nora's feelings and thoughts while she was standing at her young lover's tomb.[79]

On 4 July 1931 Joyce and Nora were married in London. They then moved to Paris, where they lived for a number of years. In December 1940 the family moved to Zurich. Joyce was ill by this time and complained of severe abdominal pains. He was hospitalised on 10 January 1941 and was diagnosed as having a perforated ulcer. An emergency operation was performed, which seemed successful at first, but a short time later he fell into a coma. He awoke briefly and asked for Nora, but lapsed into another coma. He died on 13 January 1941 and was laid to rest in the beautiful wooded Fluntern Cemetery in Zurichberg. The snow fell as Nora helped lower the coffin and then spread out her arms as if saying farewell. She lived on in Zurich, in relative poverty, and had to sell most of Joyce's manuscripts and her jewellery to survive. She died on 10 April 1951 after an illness and was buried

---

78   *Ibid.*, pp. 31, 91.
79   *Ibid.*, pp. 101–11.

some distance from her husband.[80] Their bodies were later exhumed and they were reburied together in a grave donated by the city of Zurich. A bronze memorial was unveiled over the grave on Bloomsday (the annual 16 June celebration of Joyce's life and work) in 1966.

In 1987 Joyce's short story 'The Dead' was celebrated in film. It was directed by John Huston, whose daughter, Anjelica, played the role of Gretta Conroy, while his son, Anthony, adapted the story for screen.[81]

Nora Barnacle's home in Bowling Green is now a museum dedicated to both herself and Joyce. It is owned and managed by Mary and Sheila Gallagher. The former home of Michael Bodkin is now incorporated in Richardson's Bar, Eyre Square. Information about the story is displayed in the bar. Galway Civic Trust erected a plaque commemorating the love story of Michael Bodkin and Nora Barnacle, which was unveiled on 16 June 1996 by the then mayor of Galway, Councillor Micheál Ó hUiginn, at the doorway of the old Bodkin home in Prospect Hill. It carries the following inscription:

> James Joyce's world famous short story 'The Dead' was inspired by the sad tale of his wife, Galway woman Nora Barnacle, whose first love, Michael Bodkin (Furey), lived in this building and died in 1900 'for love'.[82]

80   *Ibid.*, p. 115.
81   W. Henry, *The James Joyce Story and his Galway Connection* (Galway: Merv Griffin, 1999), pp. 1–4.
82   P. O'Dowd, 'James Joyce's "The Dead" and its Galway Connections', *Journal of the Galway Archaeological & Historical Society*, vol. 51, 1999, pp. 190, 192.

Bounds of Virtue

This is the story of the profound love that Theobald Wolfe Tone had for Elizabeth Vesey Martin. Wolfe Tone was born on 20 June 1763 in Stafford Street, Dublin (now Wolfe Tone Street). He was the son of Peter and Margaret Tone and was one of five surviving children. He showed exceptional talent in his early school days. His parents were advised to send him to a good secondary school to prepare him for Trinity College. His father was a coachbuilder, but when Tone was fifteen years old the business failed, resulting in the family moving to inherited land near Bodenstown in County Kildare. However, Tone remained in Dublin and after a chequered career in Trinity College he finally graduated in 1786. From his early years he had a burning ambition to become a soldier. He regularly visited the Phoenix Park to watch military parades and displays. He also developed a keen interest in the theatre, which was flourishing in Dublin during those years. His interest in drama led to his meeting Elizabeth Vesey Martin. She appears to have been an extraordinarily beautiful and talented woman with a great passion for the arts.[83]

Elizabeth was the wife of Sir Richard Martin, who was an MP for Galway and the owner of vast estates of

---

[83] H. Boylan, *Theobald Wolfe Tone* (Dublin: Gill & Macmillan, 1981), pp. 1–6.

land as well as being the aforementioned noted duellist who had shot a number of men whilst settling disputes.[84] Richard Martin indulged his and his wife's love of drama and set up a private theatre for amateur actors near to their Dublin home. Tone began visiting, becoming friends with Martin and infatuated with his beautiful wife. Towards the end of college term in 1782, Tone fell out of favour in Trinity because he had acted as second in a duel for an undergraduate named Anderson. Anderson had been killed and when the college authorities were informed of Tone's involvement, he was reprimanded and almost expelled. This was possibly one of the reasons for him taking a break from college in 1783. He accepted an invitation from the Martins to visit their Dangan home just outside Galway city. This was a chance for him to spend more time with Elizabeth. The Martins had no children themselves, but were looking after Richard's two half-brothers, Robert and Anthony, who were boys of twelve and thirteen. Tone acted as tutor to the boys, which meant spending much of his time at Dangan in the company of his attractive host.[85] They became close friends over a short period and Tone – now twenty years old, rather handsome, almost effeminate-looking and refined – grew increasingly attached to Elizabeth and fell passionately in love with her. He later recorded in his diary that his desire reached a degree that was almost inconceivable: 'I fell in love with a woman who made me miserable for near two years.

---

84   Barry, *An Affair of Honour*, pp. 124–5.

85   S. Lynam, *Humanity Dick Martin: 'King of Connemara' 1754–1834* (Dublin: The Lilliput Press, 1989), pp. 46–7.

I never met in history, poetry or romance, a description that came near to what I actually suffered on her account.'[86]

There is no doubt that Elizabeth loved her husband dearly. Regardless of whatever hour he arrived home from business, she would be waiting on the steps of the house to greet and embrace him. However, Richard Martin was always busy, both in his political and private life. Tone felt that Martin was neglecting his wife and as he gained her confidence he began to voice his opinion. He made comparisons, reminding Elizabeth of his attentiveness towards her and her husband's neglect.[87]

Their walks along the banks of the River Corrib, which ran close to the Martin home, must have been difficult for Tone. He was constantly in the company of this very desirable woman with whom he was so in love, yet he was careful and did not step beyond the bounds of her virtue. Elizabeth must have been aware of Tone's feelings for her.

The pair spent much time acting and rehearsing for plays together. Richard Martin had set up the Kirwan's Lane Theatre, which was located close to his townhouse on the corner of Quay Street and Cross Street, now Tigh Neachtain pub. The actual site of the theatre is not known, but it is likely to have been located at the lower end of the Cross Street entrance to Kirwan's Lane, on the left side facing the Old Dominican Convent. One of the plays Tone and Elizabeth starred in together was John Home's tragedy

---

86   'Wolfe Tone, the delightful Mrs. Martin and the theatre in Kirwan's Lane', *Galway Advertiser*, 26 November 1998.

87   Lynam, *Humanity Dick Martin*, p. 47.

Douglas, staged at Kirwan's Lane Theatre on 8 August 1783.[88] Set in Scotland during the middle ages at the time of the Danish raids, this was the most popular play of its period. Richard Martin played the role of Glenalvon, the villain, while his wife played the heroine, Lady Randolph, opposite Tone.[89]

At the time there was an ongoing feud between Martin and the notorious George Robert Fitzgerald, known as 'Fighting Fitzgerald'. Fitzgerald had shot a wolfhound belonging to Lord Altamont of Westport House, who was a good friend of Martin's. The duel that followed resulted in Martin being wounded.[90] This left the stage clear for Elizabeth and Tone for almost six months. Over time she gradually fell in love with him, returning his affections with the same ardour that he showered upon her. He also delighted at any chance of rehearsing with her, as it sometimes meant that they would have to play parts that were somewhat intimate. Tone considered Elizabeth the best actress he had ever seen, believing that she was more divine than human, and 'adored her deity'. Tone now knew that Elizabeth was in love with him and wrote in his diary, 'I preserved, as well as felt, the profoundest respect for her, she supposed she might amuse herself innocently in observing the progress of this terrible passion in the mind of an interesting young man of twenty; but this is an experiment no woman ought to make.' Even on rare occasions when they had to be apart, they employed

---

88   'Wolfe Tone, the delightful Mrs. Martin and the theatre in Kirwan's Lane'.
89   Lynam, *Humanity Dick Martin*, pp. 48–50.
90   Barry, *An Affair of Honour*, pp. 117–25.

someone to carry letters and notes to each other. Tone later admitted that Elizabeth taught him how to make himself more 'agreeable' to women.

Elizabeth announced that she was pregnant, and there was much rejoicing in the Martin household. Life was very pleasant at Dangan. However, all this changed one evening when two men, described as 'ruffians', broke into the house and attempted to arrest Martin. Tone and Martin were together in one of the rooms when the intruders arrived. Martin was confused by the incident, had no idea why it was happening and sent the men on their way. Wanting to investigate the reason for such an intrusion, he asked Tone to swear an affidavit regarding the incident, but for some unknown reason, Tone refused. Martin persisted and even threatened Tone, but he still refused, saying that it was against his principles. This resulted in Tone leaving Dangan and Elizabeth Martin, never to return. He recorded in his diary, 'Though I adored his wife beyond all humans, and knew well that my refusal was in effect a sentence of banishment from her presence for ever, I had the courage to persist in my refusal.' Thus ended 'a passion of the most extravagant violence'.[91]

Although broken-hearted, Tone moved on with his life and accepted that he would never see the woman of his most passionate desires again. However, within six months he met and fell in love with a fifteen-year-old girl, Martha (later Matilda) Witherington from Grafton Street. They eloped and were married in July 1785, and after a short

---

91   Lynam, *Humanity Dick Martin*, pp. 60–62.

honeymoon in Maynooth they returned to Dublin.[92]

Tone's life changed forever in 1791 when he helped with the foundation of the Society of United Irishmen, which originally sought parliamentary reform but later became more revolutionary. By the late 1790s the political climate in Ireland had become tense and a campaign against the United Irishmen ensued. This led to a rebellion against the British government being planned and Tone travelled to France to enlist support. The first troops sent to Ireland in 1798 sailed to Killala Bay in County Mayo. Later that year the French sent a fleet of seven frigates and a schooner under the flagship *Hoche*. In October 1798 Tone arrived off the Donegal coast on board the *Hoche*, but the English fleet had followed the French ships. Tone was in command of a battery on the gun deck and fought with utmost desperation, but after a fierce battle the guns of the *Hoche* were silenced. The captured ship was brought into Lough Swilly. Tone was dressed in a French officer's uniform and, having stepped ashore, was arrested, placed in irons and sent to Dublin for trial. On 10 November he was taken before a court martial, charged with treason and sentenced to death by hanging. Tone requested that the death sentence be carried out by firing squad, but the lord lieutenant refused. In the early hours of Monday 12 November 1798, rather than suffer the ignominious death planned for him by the authorities, Tone chose the manner in which he would die and cut his throat with a razor, which was apparently left behind by his brother, Matthew, who had already been taken out from the same cell to be hanged. Tone lingered

---

92   Boylan, *Theobald Wolfe Tone*, pp. 7–8.

on until 19 November, when he died. His body was taken by relatives and buried in the churchyard at Bodenstown, County Wicklow.[93] Through his death and ideals, Wolfe Tone became the 'Father of Irish Republicanism'. This was his legacy, and Ireland would never be the same again.[94]

It is not known how Elizabeth Martin reacted to Tone leaving Dangan, but her relationship with her husband certainly changed over the following few years. By 1790 they had three children and the family went on a continental tour, which took them to Paris. During their time there Martin was called to London on business and left Elizabeth in the city, to follow him later with the servants and their children. Shortly after Martin left, Elizabeth met a man named John Petrie and had an affair with him. In June Martin sent one of his most trusted servants to Paris to escort Elizabeth and the children to London, where he was waiting for them. When the servant, Joseph, arrived in the Paris hotel, he found Petrie and Elizabeth together. He later described Petrie as 'a small, rather ugly Englishman, much her senior'. Elizabeth Martin had, it seems, let her standards drop.

When Martin was informed of his wife's infidelity, he divorced her. He then began to wonder about Tone and Elizabeth. Questions ran through his mind. Was Tone the father of their first child?

Elizabeth did return to London, but accompanied by Petrie, and began living openly with him. However, the relationship did not last, as she died within a few years.

---

93   *Ibid.*, pp. 126–134.
94   Lynam, *Humanity Dick Martin*, pp. 114–17.

While Tone was in Paris in August 1796 he thought about Elizabeth and recorded in his journal, 'It opened my eyes to many little circumstances that passed between her and me, and perhaps (as I think now), had my passion for her been less pure, it might have been less agreeable … my ignorance of the world prevented my availing myself of opportunities which a man more trained than I would not have let slip.'[95] When Wolfe Tone's son later prepared his father's memoirs for publication, he carefully removed all references of his father's passion for Elizabeth Martin – even the statement that she had returned his affection without 'in a single instance overstepping the bounds of virtue'.[96]

The Kings Head

According to tradition, the Kings Head pub on High Street was granted to the executioner of King Charles I, who was beheaded at Whitehall on 30 January 1649.[97] For years locals and visitors have enquired about the name over the door. It has been said that Cromwell had to enlist an Irishman to execute the king as an Englishman would not carry out the deed. According to this legend, the

---

95   *Ibid.*, pp. 76–7, 99.
96   *Ibid.*, p. 274.
97   P. Cheshire, *Kings and Queens* (London: Star Fire, 2001), p. 34.

executioner was from Galway, and for his troubles he was given the inn.

To try to separate fact from myth one must look at the aftermath of the 1651–52 siege of Galway – when the city was the last to hold out against the Cromwellian conquest in Ireland – and into the life of a very volatile character named Colonel Peter Stubbers. On 12 April 1652 Colonel Stubbers led the Cromwellian army triumphantly into Galway city. He was second in command to Sir Charles Coote, the senior officer at the siege. There were to be substantial seizures of property in Galway because the authorities in Dublin had refused to ratify the Articles of Surrender.

Stubbers was appointed governor and abused his power to the extreme. The Irish and Old English Catholics were deemed a threat to the new order and many were forcibly removed from the town. During this time, the mayor and corporation were often abused violently by Cromwellian soldiers. Even the dead were not safe: many graves were uprooted and anything of value stolen, and the half-decayed corpses were left for dogs to devour.[98] Stubbers and his men also made frequent nightly raids throughout the countryside, rounding up young people for transportation to the West Indies, where they were sold as slaves.

On 25 October 1654 the Council of State ordered that the mayor and other important offices of corporation should be under the control of the 'English and Protestants'. These orders were executed immediately by the removal of the mayor, Thomas Lynch Fitz-Ambrose. Stubbers then became

---

98   Henry, *Role of Honour*, p. 75.

the first Protestant mayor of the new order in Galway. He also took possession of the mayor's house in High Street, and thus the association of the King's Head with the execution of Charles I was born. The present pub was reconstructed in the 1970s and occupies part of the original site on which the mayoral house once stood. Some portions of the internal wall structure and a fireplace still survive.

It was also believed that another Cromwellian, Richard Gunning, who lived at the rear of the High Street property, had actually carried out the execution. According to tradition, Gunning would often boast that he had 'felt the muscles on the neck of the King of England'. He frightened people, insinuating that if he could hack the head off a king he could do as he wished to any common man or woman. There is no evidence to indicate that Gunning carried out the execution other than his threatening boasts. It was rumoured that his family had plantations in the West Indies and were involved in the white slave trade. Perhaps they found a ready supplier in his friend Stubbers.

While another source states that Richard Brandon was the executioner of Charles I, it was in fact rumoured among the Cromwellians themselves that Stubbers had actually carried out the execution. There were two masked men present on the execution platform and both insisted that their identities be protected. This makes it extremely difficult to identify the actual executioner, but there are some clues. Following the Restoration of the monarchy in 1660, the Act of Indemnity introduced by Charles II pardoned all those who had supported Oliver Cromwell once they had admitted to their crimes. However, Stubbers was deliberately excluded from the terms of the act: he would not receive clemency from the new king. Stubbers was also accused of being a halberdier (an axe carrier, armed with halberd-type of battle axe) at the execution and of having signed the king's death warrant. The fact that Stubbers left his house in High Street post-Restoration and disappeared, also suggests that he feared for his survival.

The royalists ensured that the post-Restoration government had several people tried and executed for their parts in the king's death. Stubbers was in fact the only member of Cromwell's 'inner circle' to escape any form of punishment for his alleged role. Very little is known of Stubbers after this period, but it appears that he fled to Hessia, just north of Frankfurt in Germany. The Stubbers family had relatives named Hamilton living there, who later became known as the Hamilton Stubbers.

During research into the story of the Kings Head pub, it was discovered that the Hamilton family of Moyne House in Durrow, County Laois, are descendents of Peter Stubbers. It seems that they have always accepted that Stubbers was the actual executioner of the king and this story has been handed down for generations. The original building in High Street, Galway, was in the Hamilton Stubbers family until 1932, when it was finally sold. The family also maintained that Peter Stubbers returned to Ireland a number of years after his forced exile and lived quietly on the estate at Durrow.

One thing is certain: Stubbers' unwelcome arrival in Galway and his presence in the house in High Street has ensured a strong Galwegian association with the execution of the king and has added another dimension to the history of the city.

The Hole in the Wall

There is a pub in Eyre Street called the Hole in the Wall, which is very popular with young people today. The origin of the name takes one back to the smuggling trade of the eighteenth century. By that time the city walls were no longer required for defensive purposes and had been allowed to fall into ruin. Smugglers took advantage of the situation as it made their work easier, and soon large holes began to appear in the old town walls so they could bring their goods into the town without paying duty or excise on them. It seems that there was a large hole in a section of the town wall near Eyre Street through which the smugglers brought their contraband to waiting clients.

This story was passed down through generations of local people. By the late nineteenth century a thatched pub had been opened close to the site. The old town wall was no longer visible then as buildings were constructed against it. Thus the hole in the wall was blocked and consigned to memory and eventually folklore. The twentieth century saw the name Fitzgerald over the pub, and although the story was long forgotten, it was always known by its nickname: the 'hole in the wall'. The pub was in the ownership of the Fitzgerald family until the 1970s when a local businessman, Stephen Fahy, bought the property and officially named it the 'Hole in the Wall'.

Over the passage of time many people came to believe

that the hole in the wall was the stuff of legend; a fanciful story of smuggling told over a pint. However, the hole in the old city wall was exposed some twenty years ago during redevelopment work in the area. It was located almost directly behind the pub that now bears its name.[99]

The Night of the Big Wind

The night of Sunday 6 January 1839 will be forever known as the Night of the Big Wind, a night that wreaked havoc across Galway city and county, and indeed throughout the country.

In the early afternoon of that fateful Sunday the air temperature began to change, but as it was winter people were not overly concerned.[100] As darkness fell over the gas-lit streets of the city, people made their way home from evening devotions. The windows of the little houses twinkled with candlelight as people honoured the Twelfth Night of the feast of the Epiphany, or 'Little Christmas' as it is sometimes called. Children were soon tucked away in bed and the adults sat by their respective firesides to discuss the news of the day. At about 8.30 p.m. a gale began blowing from the south-west. The whistle of the wind at doorways and windows did

99   W. Henry, 'History of Galway Pubs', Information Leaflet, 2001.
100   Editor, 'The Night of the Big Wind', *Ireland's Own*, 15 January 1999.

not alarm people: after all, they were living in close proximity to the sea and were used to strong winds and storms.

However, this was somewhat different. As each hour passed the fury of the howling wind increased and began to rattle the doors and windows of houses. Inside, people prayed and sprinkled holy water in the hope that they might be spared the devastation of the storm. By 11.00 p.m. the wind was raging with all the force of a hurricane. The power of the gusts was such that it ripped slates from the roofs of houses and hurled them great distances, crashing into the streets and lanes of the town. The masonry supporting chimney stacks and the parapets of many buildings could not withstand the violence of the storm and began to crumple, with chimneys and roofs collapsing into the streets. Debris was crashing through the windows of houses, causing widespread panic.[101] People huddled together in their humble dwellings, many afraid to remain but too terrified to move. To leave their homes could mean being swept away by the violent force of the wind; to stay could also be risking death. The terror was such that many people felt that their last hour had come. The slates and masonry continued to fly in all directions. As roofs were carried away, men, women and children screamed and cried as they scurried for shelter. There are recorded accounts of people being unable to stand and crawling to safety. Seven people lost their lives in the city that night and many more were seriously injured.[102]

---

101 'The Night of the Big Wind', *Brat Muire/The Mantle*, no. 55–6, 1971, pp. 28–29.

102 'Tremendous and Frightful Hurricane', *The Galway Weekly Advertiser and Connaught Journal*, 12 January 1839.

In Mainguard Street, Catherine Reid and her sister Mrs Callanan were killed when their house collapsed on top of them and they were buried in the rubble. Another woman, Mrs Gorman, lost her life in Eyre Street. A Mrs Shaughnessy, seeking shelter in Shop Street, was killed by falling masonry. Jim Healy of Lombard Street was struck by a stone from a chimney stack and killed, while flying slates killed Ann Morris and Mary Keane. Hundreds more were injured, and four other people died from wounds received on the dreadful night. The storm raged until about 5 a.m. and only then did it begin to die down, but by this time it had devastated many buildings in the town.

The sight that greeted the people as the morning sky brightened resembled a sacked city. People could be forgiven for thinking that huge cannons had been fired in an attempt to destroy the town. Every building bore marks of a great calamity. Many buildings were completely stripped of slates and glass. Entire houses and in some cases even whole streets were destroyed. Lanes were covered in broken masonry, glass and slates. Even the County Court House had not escaped – all its windows were smashed and the roof was destroyed. The County Infirmary at Prospect Hill, where some people had sought refuge and where many of the injured had been taken, was also left without its windows or roof. However, one section of this building escaped almost undamaged, and it was there that many of the wounded were cared for by a local doctor named Blake. He did exceptional work under the circumstances, performing various operations, including amputations, in an effort to save lives. In some cases he was forced to use whiskey as an anaesthetic. Although four of his patients later died, he did manage to save many others.

While conditions on land were horrendous, the situation for those at sea was even worse. Three boats had sailed out from Galway docks on the morning of the storm, destined for Carraroe and Rosmuc. They were caught in the raging sea and no trace of the twenty-three people on board these vessels was ever found. All were presumed drowned. Most of the fishing vessels at Long Walk and Galway docks were battered against the quay walls and were either sunk or reduced to driftwood. Seven coastal steamers broke their moorings and were driven out to sea, to be carried back by high, raging waves and smashed on the rocks near Forthill, Renmore and Ballyloughane.

The entire western seaboard and midlands took the brunt of the hurricane. Scenes of devastation greeted people throughout the countryside. Scarcely a house in Salthill escaped damage. Fire had always been a danger with open hearths, thatched roofs and the enormous wind to fan the flames, and it destroyed 103 houses in Loughrea, while 20 houses in Oranmore suffered the same fate.[103] Many thatched cabins of the poor along the seafront were also destroyed and the contents of haggards were strewn for miles around. Providence did not spare the mighty either: many of the gentry also suffered, their residences falling victim to the storm. The great manor houses of Castlehackett, Furbo and Tyrone, and even Cregg Castle, were all damaged. The occupants of Ross House in Connemara, the Martin

---

103 'Night of the Big Wind', pp. 28–9.

family, gathered in the basement in total terror. Before retreating to the cellar, Mr Martin, while listening to the raging winds outside, looked up at the vaulted ceiling and commented, 'If Ross falls, not a house in Ireland will stand.' Ross survived, but evidence of the violence it experienced was everywhere when the family emerged from their place of refuge the following morning. Off-white frothy foam covered much of the lawn, blown in from the sea many miles distant.

Thousands of trees fell that night, over 130,000 alone on two estates in Mayo. Almost every tree in Garbally Park, County Galway, was uprooted, many of them hundreds of years old. Thousands of birds were killed, ripped from their nests and hurled into every object in the path of the storm. Churches all over the diocese suffered untold damage. St Patrick's Church in Forster Street had its roof torn off, as did the neighbouring houses in the avenues and streets close by.

Many thousands of people were left homeless and it took years to repair the destruction. In the countryside, the storm ended the era of the mud cabin forever, as people began to rebuild in stone. The country people were used to hard times through hunger, disease and poverty, but this storm brought additional suffering. Throughout Ireland, the death toll of that dreadful night reached almost 300. In Galway, things could have been worse had a spring tide accompanied the hurricane, as was sometimes the case at that time of year. The town would have experienced a rising and raging sea, causing much more destruction. Nevertheless, the Night of the Big Wind was the worst-known natural disaster to hit

Galway and lived on in folk memory well into the twentieth century.[104]

Mary McManus, Virgin, 1827

T he Blake family of Galway built Merlin Park House in 1812. Great festivities were held when the family moved into the house, and many of the leading gentry of the day attended. It seems that the party continued for a week, setting the pace for the coming years. Over time the family employed a number of people, including a servant girl named Mary McManus. There is no record of her age when she began working for the Blakes, but perhaps she was fourteen or fifteen years old, similar to other servant girls starting work for the first time during that period.

Tragedy struck during one of the famous parties in 1827 and Mary was killed. There are two versions of the story about how she met her death. One relates that she fell backwards down a stairway and struck her head off the stone tiles at the bottom of the stairs. The other account states that she was leaning over a banister trying to view the footman and a house maid cuddling up together in a corner. It seems that Mary leaned out too far, lost her balance and fell to her death on the stone tiles beneath. Rather than

104 'Tremendous and Frightful Hurricane'.

upset the guests, her death was hushed up so the party could continue.

Again, there are two versions of what happened next: the first account states that she was immediately buried in the basement of the building and her grave was later marked with a flagstone, which was simply inscribed, 'Mary McManus, Virgin, 1827'. According to the second story, she was quickly buried in the woods close to the house, with the same inscribed flagstone later marking her grave.

Merlin Park House eventually came into the hands of Captain Wyndham Waithman, the senior recruiting officer for Galway during the Great War of 1914–18, and his wife. The house was purchased through acquisition in 1945 and demolished to make way for the new sanatorium, now known as Merlin Park Hospital. Captain Waithman obviously knew the story of Mary McManus as he made some enquiries when the work was completed, asking the workmen if they had found any bones during the demolition work. However, nothing was reported. Mrs Waithman later claimed that she had seen the inscribed flagstone in the basement. However, Norman White, the architect who designed Merlin Park sanatorium, gave strict instructions that the location of the grave was to be cordoned off and not interfered with, which would indicate that Mary McManus was buried in the woods.

The use of the term 'Virgin' on the flagstone would indicate that she was not married.[105]

---

105   N. Sheerin, 'The Short Life of Mary McManus', *Renmore Seagull*, vol. 15, no. 3, December 2010, p. 7.

The Crimean Cannons

Throughout the late nineteenth and twentieth centuries two large 36-pounder Russian cannons stood in Eyre Square. They were removed to a new location at City Hall in College Road during the re-development of the park in 2003. These guns were among the weaponry captured during the Crimean War of 1854–6. According to some sources, they were captured on 5 November 1854 at the Battle of Inkerman, but they are more likely to have been taken after the siege of Sebastopol. They were presented to Galway by the British War Department for its support during the war, and, it has been stated, largely in honour of the courage and dedication to duty of the Connaught Rangers.[106] This regiment was involved in all the major actions of this war and was made up of men mainly from the west of Ireland, with Galway being well represented among its ranks.

The guns were shipped from Woolwich Arsenal on board the *Lady Eglinton*. There was great excitement when the cannons arrived in Galway in 1857 and hundreds of curious onlookers turned out to see these nineteenth-century weapons of mass destruction. The town commissioners had organised a handing-over ceremony. Described as 'The Sebastopol Trophies', the cannons were officially

---

106 W. Henry, 'The Cannons at Eyre Square', *St Patrick's Parish Magazine*, 1997, pp. 20–23.

presented to Galway at midday on 3 August 1857 amid pouring rain.[107] The guns were mounted on iron carriages and taken in procession to the Railway Hotel (now the Hotel Meyrick). The High Sheriff, Peter Sarsfield Comyn, led the procession, with a detachment of marines taking up the rear.[108] The guns were placed on plinths located on each side of the main entrance to the hotel. The marines fired off three volleys of rifle fire before the speeches started. The heavy rain continued and the various speakers hurriedly addressed the crowd, keeping the ceremony as short as possible. This was followed by the town commissioners extending an invitation to all present to a reception in the Town Hall, where food and refreshments were provided. Musical entertainment was provided by a German brass band. Some hours later, the rain cleared and there was a fireworks display held at Eyre Square.

These guns had poured out death and destruction in a brutal war that had shocked the public. It was possibly the first time that gruesome, rather than glorious, reports of war reached the public. The reports came via the pen of William Russell, the notable war correspondent. In 1866 the guns were removed to Custume Military Barracks in Athlone because the government feared that the Fenians, who were dedicated to the establishment of an independent Irish Republic, might attempt to re-service them and use them against the crown. While the British believed that this was

107 T. Collins, 'The Town Hall in 1857 – When Galway Hospitality Met Crimean Cannon', *Journal of the Galway Archaeological & Historical Society*, vol. 48, 1996, pp. 138–9.
108 'The Sebastopol Trophies', *The Galway Vindicator*, 5 August 1857.

a real threat, others pointed out that the fears were totally unfounded: how could rebels using guerrilla tactics be in a position to use heavy siege guns, even if they could have them serviced? Common sense prevailed and the cannons were returned in 1868, but this time to a new location at the northern end of Eyre Square.[109]

It has been estimated that some 4,000 Russian cannons of various types were captured by the British during the Crimean War and later distributed throughout the empire. Some people believed that this was a show of power on the part of the British and acted as a warning to would-be revolutionaries. However, others said that by distributing and displaying the weapons, they were in a sense trying to justify the appalling casualties suffered during the war. Both the Galway guns have the double-headed eagle of Imperial Russia in relief and display the maker's number. They are similar to the cannons used to produce the Victoria Cross, and there has been a suggestion that some of these guns were in fact of Chinese origin and were captured by the Russians near Canton during the first Opium War of 1839–42. Nevertheless, the cannons are now an important part of Galway's social history, with generations of locals and visitors having their photographs taken sitting on or beside these symbols of a long-forgotten war.[110]

---

109   Collins, 'The Town Hall', pp. 139, 141.
110   Henry, 'Cannons at Eyre Square', pp. 20–23.

Anach Cuain

The worst recorded drowning tragedy in the history of the River Corrib occurred on Thursday 4 September 1828. It is remembered in song by the lonely lament 'Anach Cuain', penned by the celebrated blind poet Anthony Raftery. Early that fateful morning people gathered at Annaghdown Pier to go to the fair at Fair Hill in the Claddagh. At the time people living in Annaghdown who wished to travel to Galway had no choice but to use the river, as the Headford road had not been built. The boat began making its way slowly across the lower lake of the Corrib loaded with ten sheep, a quantity of lumber and thirty-one passengers. The boat was overloaded, but having made the journey on many occasions, this was not a concern for most people on board. As the boat approached the Menlo area a sheep put its leg through one of the old planks in the bottom of the boat and in an attempt to stem the water that began leaking into the boat, one of the passengers placed his coat in the aperture and stamped on it. The plank gave way under the pressure. Water gushed up into the boat and it immediately began to sink. Panic erupted as the sinking vessel quickly filled with water and became submerged. Many of the people found themselves in a hopeless situation as they were unable to swim. Within minutes, nineteen people had lost their lives. There was another boat in the area at the time and it managed to rescue twelve people from the river. Upon hearing of the disaster, Major Dickson and members of his 64th Regiment, stationed in Galway at the time, went to assist, but it was too late.[111]

One report stated that the accident occurred opposite Bushy Park while another claimed it was opposite Menlo Cemetery. The actual location of the tragedy was later identified as occurring between the two white-stone beacons at the junction of the Old River and the Friars Cut, the new water course to the lake.

On 6 September 1828 an account of the disaster was published in *The Galway Weekly Advertiser and Connaught Journal* and described the boat as 'an old row boat, in a rotten and leaky condition' that should not have been in service. It also confirmed that the boat was overloaded, which contributed to the loss of life. It seems that eighteen of the nineteen bodies were recovered by the following day. The coroner, John Blakeney, held an inquest in the immediate aftermath of the tragedy. James O'Hara, MP, and the mayor of Galway, James Hardiman Burke, also attended. Despite the condition of the boat and the fact that it was overloaded, the jury returned a verdict of accidental drowning.[112] The tragedy caused much heartbreak in the locality and has lived on in the memory of the local people, passed down from one generation to another with the aid of Raftery's poignant poem.

---

111 'Most Deplorable Accident – Nineteen Persons Drowned!!!', *The Galway Weekly Advertiser and Connaught Journal*, 6 September 1828.

112 M. Semple, *Reflections on Lough Corrib* (Maurice Semple, 1974), pp. 153–7.

The Hag's Walk

There is a narrow, rough path of stones stretching out into the lower Lough Corrib near Angliham that is known locally as the Hag's Walk. This narrow causeway is covered by the lake for most of the year and is not visible. However, it lies just beneath the surface of the water, and many an angler and fisherman have cursed it, having run their boats onto the hidden stones. It can be seen on clear days from the fields overlooking the lake. On rare occasions people walk out along it. Depending on the angle of the view from shore, one could be forgiven for thinking that the person was walking on water. Tradition tells us that an old hag who lived in this area centuries ago constructed it. It seems that she had a sister, also an old hag, who lived on the other side of the lake. There was much trouble between them and they were always fighting and exchanging insults. This resulted in the hag living near Angliham constructing the causeway in an effort to get across the lake and attack her sister ... hence the name.[113]

---

113 Interview: Tom Small, 20 May 2006.

The *Hugo de Groot*

A t 4.05 a.m. on Thursday 14 August 1958, the Dutch KLM Airliner *Hugo de Groot* flew out of Shannon Airport. The super-constellation aircraft was en route from Amsterdam via Shannon, bound for Gander in Newfoundland. There were ninety-one passengers and eight crew members on board flight 607-E. The aircraft checked in with Shannon when it reached 12,000 feet. The last radio contact with the *Hugo de Groot* was at 4.40 a.m., when the Shannon air traffic controller requested her captain to relay a message to another aircraft regarding its flight course. The captain replied that he had contacted the other aircraft and received an acknowledgment. The Shannon air traffic controller thanked him. At that time the plane was approximately 120 nautical miles west-north-west of Shannon.[114]

Sometime later flight 607-E failed to make a routine radio check with Shannon and the alarm was raised immediately, sending the air and sea rescue services into action. Gander airport was also contacted, and they stated that they had been in contact with the aircraft. However, two hours later, they cancelled this message. RAF rescue planes were scrambled and shipping in the area was notified. Just after midday an RAF plane sighted wreckage and bodies about sixty miles

---

114 'Inquest and Funeral of the Air Crash Victims', *The Connacht Tribune*, 23 August 1958.

William Henry

west of the Aran Islands. Ships in the vicinity were requested to proceed immediately to the crash site. Ten ships responded, among them the *Naomh Eanna, Kilronan, General Leclerc* and the Canadian destroyer *Crusader*. When the ships reached the area they found numerous bodies scattered over about a mile radius. The first ships to arrive began the gruesome task of recovering the bodies. One vessel took on board five female victims, all of whom had been mortally wounded and were not wearing life jackets. This could indicate that whatever caused the disaster happened suddenly. The captain of the *Naomh Eanna* reported that the area was littered with debris. Among the items they recovered was a gent's watch belonging to a man named Paul Christovik, one of the victims. It had stopped at 4.48 a.m., just minutes after the last radio message with Shannon, and possibly an indication of when the disaster occurred.

Meanwhile, in Galway city the staff of the Regional Hospital (now Galway University Hospital) and local units of the Red Cross and Order of Malta were alerted. They all prepared to receive bodies. Some believed that there might be survivors; however, as evening wore on, all hope faded for the ninety-nine passengers and crew of the ill-fated flight.[115] Thirty-four bodies were eventually recovered, nine male and twenty-five female; one, a little baby girl, Bernadette Kock Van Leeuwen, was just fourteen months old. At about 6.30 p.m. on Friday the first mercy ships began arriving at Galway docks, watched by a huge, silent crowd. The French

---

115 'Air Disaster Remains Will Arrive in Galway', *The Connacht Tribune*, 16 August 1958.

118

trawler *Jules Verne* led them. Units of the Red Cross, Order of Malta, Fire Brigade and the Civil Defence Corps met the ships. The bodies were removed and taken to the hospital, where Dutch and Irish doctors worked throughout the night carrying out post-mortems.

Earlier that day, KLM officials and Dutch government investigators had arrived in Galway. They began sifting through the meagre pieces of wreckage for clues to try to identify the cause of the disaster. The inquest opened on 18 August in the Great Southern Hotel, Eyre Square, and eleven people were called to give evidence. Deputy Coroner W. B. Allen took the chair. The hearing lasted five hours, after which a verdict was delivered. It was declared that the causes of death were 'multiple injuries, fractures and haemorrhages due to the violent impact'. According to the report, there was no evidence to show the actual cause of the disaster. The findings of the inquest were reported across Europe and the United States by reporters from the major news agencies attending. Only twelve of the victims were positively identified.

On the afternoon of Tuesday 19 August, Galway city mourned when the remains of twenty-three victims of the air crash were brought to the New Cemetery for burial. Catholic, Protestant, Presbyterian, Jewish, Muslim and Greek Orthodox representatives were all included in the religious services held in the grounds of the hospital before the funeral cortège moved off. The service was also attended by government representatives from the nations of those who had been on board – America, Argentina, Ireland, Egypt, Mexico, Great Britain, the United Arab

Republic and, of course, Holland. The funeral cortège, the biggest ever seen in the city, consisted of a fleet of hearses and five army trucks. Soldiers of An Céad Cath Battalion acted as pall bearers. Thousands of people lined the route to the cemetery and there was an unforgettable sympathetic silence among them. All businesses along the route of the funeral closed as a mark of respect. Along the Bohermore road leading to the cemetery, mothers and children knelt in prayer as the coffins passed.[116] A mass grave had been excavated on the eastern side, just inside the main gates of the cemetery. Upon arrival, soldiers began to lay the coffins in rows along the grave site in preparation for burial. Following the graveside ceremony, the coffins were covered with earth. Stone memorials were later placed over the site of each coffin, many simply reading 'Unidentified'. A large stone memorial was also erected over the mass grave and a path was constructed around the boundary of the grave site.

The youngest victim, little Bernadette Kock Van Leeuwen, whose parents also perished in the disaster, was buried on Friday 29 August close to the communal grave of the other victims. Several hundred children, members of the Red Cross, Order of Malta, nurses and many dignitaries attended the funeral. Bernadette's remains were later laid to rest in her own country, as were some of the other victims.[117] *The Connacht Tribune* reported on 23 August that the loss of

---

116 'Inquest and Funeral'.
117 'Youngest Air Crash Victim Laid to Rest', *The Connacht Tribune*, 30 August 1958.

the super-constellation was the worst civil airline disaster involving a single aircraft in the history of aviation.

The loss of the *Hugo de Groot* remains a mystery today and many questions are still unanswered. The pathologist at the Regional Hospital, Dr J. D. Kennedy, said that in his opinion there was no evidence of an explosion. However, while the bodies showed evidence of being immersed in the sea, there was no evidence of drowning. All of the victims showed evidence of trauma. The main type of injury was reported to be that of a high-speed impact, yet there was no collision with another aircraft. Many of the victims were not wearing life jackets, which would surely be the first priority if an aircraft were in danger of ditching in the sea. Why was there no distress call? Why did Gander airport report that they had been in contact with the *Hugo de Groot* when responding to the alert from Shannon and two hours later cancel this message?[118] Perhaps there is more evidence waiting to be discovered.

At the time of the disaster, Peter Greene was the mayor of Galway and was involved in supporting family members and the investigators arriving in the town in the wake of the crash. Two years later, he was among a number of recipients who were awarded the Insignia of the Order of Orange-Nassau by Queen Juliana of Holland in recognition of their support and services following the loss of the *Hugo de Groot*. The Dutch Ambassador to Ireland, Dr Kasteel, formally presented the insignia to Greene in the Great Southern

---

118 'Inquest and Funeral'.

Hotel.[119] On 14 August 2008 Galway City Council held a commemoration ceremony for all those who died on the *Hugo de Groot* fifty years earlier.

On 15 August 1949 another aircraft crashed into the sea close to the Aran Islands resulting in the deaths of eight people. Fifty survivors were brought to Galway for treatment.[120]

A Saintly Visit

O liver Plunkett was born on 1 November 1625 in Loughcrew, County Meath. He was educated under the care of his kinsman, Dr Patrick Plunkett, Abbot of St Mary's in Dublin.[121] While still in his early teens Plunkett travelled to Rome, where he settled into a scholarly existence of study. Apparently he did not intend to return to Ireland, but this changed when the exiled archbishop of Armagh died in 1669. Pope Clement IX appointed Plunkett as his successor.[122] Plunkett's duties brought him to Galway in the spring of 1673, when he arrived to confirm the pallium (an

119 Henry, *Role of Honour*, p. 131.
120 'Island and Sea Service', *The Connacht Tribune*, 23 August 1958.
121 'Blessed Oliver Plunkett', *Brat Muirel The Mantle*, no. 2, 1958.
122 H. P. Montague, *The Saints and Martyrs of Ireland* (Buckinghamshire: Colin Smythe, 1981), pp. 67–9.

ecclesiastical vestment bestowed on certain individuals by
the pope to symbolise jurisdiction delegated by the Holy
See) on Archbishop James Lynch of Tuam. During his stay,
Plunkett visited the Dominicans in St Mary's Church in the
Claddagh, which very much impressed him, as did Galway
and its people.[123] The following is an extract from a letter
written by Oliver Plunkett following his visit:

> The city of Galway, although small, is very beautiful, and
> two-thirds of the people are Catholics, but very poor because
> they have been deprived of all source of revenue. Oh, what a
> devout and hospitable people! They maintain three religious
> houses, one of the Dominican, another of the Augustinian
> and a third of the Franciscan. The Dominicans have the
> finest and most ornate church in this country, and all three
> communities have always lived exemplary observance. The
> city is very strong – it is a sea-port, and it was the last in the
> whole country to be attacked by Cromwell and it held out
> for a long time. The Superior, or as they call him, the Warden
> of the secular clergy in Galway and nine or ten neighbouring
> parishes, claims exemption from the jurisdiction of the
> archbishop [of Tuam] …[124]

One can see from this account that Plunkett also recognised
the suffering of the impoverished people of Galway.

In 1678 Titus Oates and his anti-Catholic propaganda
co-author Israel Tonge concocted the so-called 'Popish
Plot' – a fictitious conspiracy about a Catholic plot to kill
King Charles II – which caused widespread anti-Catholic
hysteria and anti-Irish paranoia. While Oates and Tonge's

---

123 E. Ó hEideain, *The Dominicans in Galway 1241–1991* (Galway: The
Dominican Priory, 1991), p. 28.
124 'Blessed Oliver Plunkett', p. 34.

fabrication continued no prominent Catholic was safe, and some thirty-five people were executed.[125] The authorities suspected Oliver Plunkett of supporting and plotting a French invasion, resulting in him being arrested and put on trial. The court in Ireland failed to convict him so he was then transferred to England. One of the crown witnesses was Florence Mac Moyer, the last hereditary keeper of the ninth-century Latin manuscript the *Book of Armagh*. This time Plunkett was found guilty and was hung, drawn and quartered at Tyburn on 1 July 1681, the last Catholic to be martyred there. His body is buried at the Benedictine Abbey at Downside, England, and his head is now displayed in Drogheda Cathedral.[126] Oliver Plunkett was beatified in 1920, and canonised in 1975. He was the first Irishman to be granted sainthood since Laurence O'Toole of Dublin in 1226.[127]

Jordan's Island

Jordan's Island is located close to the Quincentennial Bridge, one of the busiest routes over the River Corrib, and just opposite the ruin of Terryland Castle. Following

125 R. Castleden, *British History: A Chronological Dictionary of Dates* (London: Parragon, 1994), p. 139.
126 Montague, *Saints and Marytrs*, pp. 70–71.
127 Crealey, *An Irish Almanac*, pp. 27, 88, 132.

the surrender of Galway to the Cromwellians in 1652, a radical Protestant sect called (by their detractors) the Anabaptists arrived in Galway.[128] The name 'Anabaptists' derives from the Greek for 'to baptise again' and refers to the sect's practice of baptising adults rather than babies. The Anabaptists' adherence to believers' baptism, which they believed was the only form of baptism authorised by scripture, led to their condemnation and persecution by both Catholics and Protestants, who believed that adult baptism constituted a second ceremony.

Anabaptist communities were modelled on early Christian communities: they were devout believers of their tradition and dedicated to leading a saintly life in strict accordance with the teachings of scripture. As such, they practised full submersion baptism of adults in Galway, in accordance with Jesus' adult baptism in the River Jordan. The place they chose to carry out these ceremonies was the narrow stretch of river in front of Terryland Castle, located between the riverbank and a small island, which they named Jordan's Island, after the River Jordan. It is believed that the Cromwellians became frustrated with the Anabaptists after a time and this was one of the reasons why that religious group left Galway.[129]

---

128 P. O'Dowd, 'The History of Galway', lecture to the Galway Archaeological & Historical Society, 12 June 1993.

129 O'Dowd, 'The History of Galway'.

Tom 'The Moor' Molineaux

Tom 'The Moor' Molineaux was an African–American champion boxer who died in Galway almost 200 years ago. Tom was born in 1784 on a slave plantation in Virginia, USA. He came from a family of fighters and was involved in the sport from a young age. According to tradition, Tom was a strong youth, a tough boxer and over time he fought his way to freedom.

He arrived in England in about 1809, defeated two challengers there and laid claim to the heavyweight title by challenging the celebrated British champion Tom Cribb. The fight took place in December 1810 and was the first inter-racial fight for an international title. The brutal fight took place outside in terrible conditions of 'chilling rain' and heavy wind. At the end of thirty-three rounds, Molineaux was forced to concede defeat, having being 'badly battered' to the ground. He had nothing left to give, was in a stupor from the punches and said to his second, Bill Richmond, 'Me can fight no more.' Although he had won the title, Cribb was forced into temporary retirement because of the severe beating he had suffered at the hands of Molineaux.

Molineaux did fight again, but had to try to coax Cribb out of retirement and into a rematch. To encourage this, Molineaux issued a general challenge to anyone in England to fight him. The challenge was taken up by the intervening champion, Joe Rimmer, who lost the ensuing fight, making

Molineaux heavyweight champion. Tom Cribb was thus forced to accept Molineaux's second challenge if he were to regain the title. The fight took place exactly one year after the first match. The second great battle, which took place in September 1811, was staged in an eight-metre ring before a huge crowd of 25,000 people in Thistleton Gap, Leicester. Molineaux fought hard, but Cribb wore him down, and after a vicious assault in the eleventh round, the old champion regained the title.[130]

Nevertheless, 'The Moor' still wasn't finished with boxing and sometime between 1816 and 1817 he arrived in Dublin to take up any contest. He joined a group of boxers who were travelling throughout Ireland giving exhibition bouts and issuing challenges. It was while engaged in this activity that he eventually arrived in Galway. At that time there was strong support for boxing in Galway and fighters visited the town from time to time. In fact, boxers from various parts of England and the United States included the City of the Tribes amongst their boxing venues.

While in Galway, Tom Molineaux contracted influenza and became very ill. He died on 4 August 1818 and was buried in St James Cemetery, Mervue. The exact location of the grave is unknown, but it is believed to be somewhere in the centre. [131]

---

130 S. Andre and N. Fleischer, *A Pictorial History of Boxing* (London: Hamlyn, 1985), pp. 26–8.

131 Sheerin, *Renmore and its Environs*, pp. 104–6.

The Galway Independent Volunteers and Militia

On 31 May 1779 the Galway Independent Volunteers were formed. They consisted of about 400 well-disciplined troops, divided into six battalions and two companies. Sir Richard Martin of Dangan was the first colonel. While Martin had never been a soldier, his reputation for courage plus his aforementioned skill with both a sword and pistol was renowned and made him a good choice for the position. The commanding officers included Colonel Martin, Lieutenant-Colonel James Shee, Major John Blake, Captain James O'Hara (Grenadier Company), Captain Mark Lynch (Battalion Company) and Captain Michael Blake (Light Infantry).

One of the main objectives of the Volunteers was the liberation of parliament through the abolition of Poynings' Law, also known as the 1495 Poynings' Act, which had placed the Irish parliament under the authority of the parliament of England. As they felt it was their patriotic duty to wear clothes that were manufactured in Ireland, family members of the Volunteers decided to boycott the purchase of wool, cotton, silken goods, refined sugar and porter that were not of Irish origin. Soon Volunteer corps all over the country followed Galway's example.[132]

---

132 S. McGuire, 'Galway and the Irish Volunteers', *Galway Reader*, vol. 2, nos 1, 2, 1949–50, pp. 87–9.

The Saturday market, Galway (Valentine & Sons Ltd).
Tommy Holohan Collection

Claddagh fishing boats, Galway (Valentine & Sons Ltd).
Tommy Holohan Collection

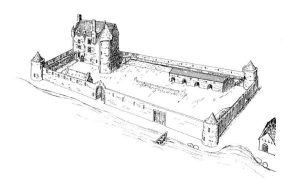

Conjectural drawing of Terryland Castle. *(Courtesy of the late Peggy Dooley)*

St Augustine's Well, Lough Atalia. *(Author's Collection)*

Mutton Island lighthouse. *(After James Hardiman, 1820)*

The Spanish Armada memorial plaque. *(Author's Collection)*

Nora Barnacle's house, Bowling Green. *(Author's Collection)*

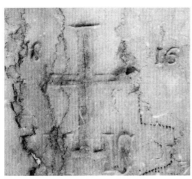

1816 cross, Galway Court House. *(Author's Collection)*

Sienna tile, Bowling Green. *(Author's Collection)*

Lime kiln, Fishery Field. *(Author's Collection)*

'The Hanging of the Bodkin Murderers' by Eamonn O'Regan. *(Courtesy of Eamonn O'Regan)*

The Kings Head Pub. *(Author's Collection)*

Burial of the KLM air disaster victims, 1958. *(Courtesy of Patrick Craven)*

The Sliding
Rock,
Shantalla.
*(Author's
Collection)*

Gavin Duffy and David O'Brien
located the milestone at Roscam
2001. *(Author's Collection)*

Sketch of Martin Reilly by
Éamonn Ceannt. *(Courtesy of
the Allen Library)*

Menlo Castle on the morning of the fire, 26 July 1910.
(Courtesy of Jonathan Margetts)

The Christopher Columbus monument, a gift from the people of Genoa to Galway. *(Author's Collection)*

The Crusader's Tomb, St Nicholas' Collegiate Church. *(Author's Collection)*

Old County Infirmary building. *(Courtesy of Arthur McWilliams)*

Nun's Island distillery. *(Author's Collection)*

Merlin Park Castle. *(Author's Collection)*

Italian Madonna of the Rosary in the Claddagh church. *(Author's Collection)*

Merchant's mark on the right and the Lynch coat of arms on the left in William Street. *(Author's Collection)*

St Augustine's Fort.
(after James Hardiman, 1820)

The Daggered Heart symbol carved into the top of a wall at Nimmo's Pier, Claddagh. *(Author's Collection)*

Mothers meeting, Eglington Street, Galway *circa* 1901. *(Author's Collection)*

While they had initial success, the lifespan of the Volunteers was relatively short. The French Revolution of 1789 unsettled the establishment in England and indeed Ireland, and the increased hostilities between England and France that culminated in war breaking out in 1793 led to the introduction of the Militia Act, which introduced partial conscription, in 1793. Outbreaks of Whiteboyism – the Whiteboys were an underground Irish agrarian organisation that employed violent tactics to defend the rights of tenant farmers – and further Catholic relief acts also played a role in the Militia Act's passing. The Galway Volunteers felt threatened by the subsequent establishment of a new military force and voiced their concerns at the general meeting of the Volunteers held on 23 December 1793 at the Coffee-House Tavern in Galway. During proceedings the Volunteer leadership stated that they were adequate to preserve the peace and tranquillity of the town themselves. They also took this opportunity to pledge their total loyalty to the crown.

However, the English parliament believed the Volunteers were outside the control of the establishment. The formation of the counteractive Galway Militia and another regiment, the Connaught Rangers, went ahead, and signalled the end for the Volunteers. The Galway Volunteers were not totally lost as a fighting force, though, as many of them joined the Connaught Rangers and were welcomed into the ranks of the new regiment.[133]

---

133   D. C. A. Wilkins, 'Defence Prepared: The Galway Militia from 1793', *Journal of the Galway Archaeological & Historical Society*, vol. 50, 1998, pp. 38–40.

The militia headquarters, during the early days, was in Ballinasloe, possibly because the commander was the Earl of Clancarty, whose family home was at Garbally, close to the town. Galway became the 11th Regiment of the Irish Militia. The militia could be considered a national force as most of its officers were Irish.[134]

One of them, Captain and Adjutant Charles le Poer Trench, was stationed at Loughrea from 1797 to 1799. His actual title was the Honourable and Venerable Charles le Poer Trench, Archdeacon of Ardagh, but this clergyman is better known to history as 'Skin-Him-Alive Trench' for his cruelty. While Trench was stationed at Loughrea, the wife of a Galway trooper was accused of stealing two brass candlesticks. There was no trial: he simply had the woman tied by her hands and feet to a triangle in the barracks square before the assembled regiment. He ordered that first she be stripped, but the woman struggled violently when the drum-major attempted to carry out the orders. Trench then 'cursed and damned' the woman and struck the soldier with a stick because he had failed to rip her clothes off. Trench again told the soldier to carry out his orders, but this time to use a knife to cut the woman's clothing. She was then stripped to the waist and flogged in full view of the regiment. Her husband was present and fainted upon seeing his wife receive fifty lashes. The humiliation did not end there, for when the physical punishment was completed, the unfortunate woman was drummed out of the barrack yard

---

134 *Ibid.*, pp. 37–41.

to the tune of the 'Rogue's March'.[135]

Another well-known figure of the Galway Militia was Colonel Giles Eyre, a third cousin of Charles le Poer Trench, but very different by character and nature. Colonel Eyre spent large sums of money on uniforms for the men under his command and the Galway Militia became one of the best-dressed regiments in Ireland.[136]

In addition to its home defence role, the militia performed several other duties, such as escorting mail coaches to protect them from highwaymen, watching over bailiffs and coastguards and preventing illicit distilling. Most of these duties later became the responsibilities of the police. The closest the regiment ever came to action in war was in 1796, with the threat of a French invasion. From 1816 the militia went into a slow decline and orders were issued that vacancies were not to be filled. By the late 1820s the Galway Militia was costing the War Office in London almost £24,000 per annum. Nevertheless, it survived and was popular among the people of Galway. The fact that it was in existence for over another sixty years indicates that volunteers were still being accepted into its ranks.

During the eighteenth and nineteenth centuries, the band of the Galway Militia provided twice-weekly entertainment at Eyre Square. They even advertised their performances to

---

135 S. McGuire, 'Ballinasloe – The Flogging Parson: Honourable and Venerable Charles Le Poer Trench, Archdeacon of Ardagh', *Galway Reader*, vol. 3, nos 1, 2, 1950, p. 97.

136 I. Gantz, *Signpost to Eyrecourt: Portrait of the Eyre Family Triumphant in the Cause of Liberty Derbyshire, Wiltshire, Galway c. 1415–1856* (Bath: Kingsmead Press, 1975), pp. 183, 188.

ensure a large attendance. On 19 October 1855 the militia paraded in the square for the presentation of the colours by Lady Clanricarde. The militia was then under the command of her husband, Lord Clanricarde. Lord Dunlo commanded the guard of honour. At the closing of the ceremony, Lady Clanricarde took centre stage and addressed an 800-strong battalion of soldiers as hundreds of people gathered to watch the spectacle. To celebrate the presentation of colours, Lord and Lady Clanricarde held a ball at the Railway Hotel that night. All military ranks from Galway, Mayo, Clare and King's County (Offaly) attended. 'Beautiful ladies' dressed in the latest fashions of the day were present and danced the night away to the sound of the great European composers. No expense was spared for the event and it was hailed for many years as the most successful ball ever held in Galway.

The Haldane Army Reforms of 1881 resulted in the Galway Militia becoming the 4th Volunteer Battalion of the 88th Foot of Connaught Rangers, thus ending another phase in the military history of Galway.[137]

The Railway Children

Hidden away beneath the Bohermore road is a huge railway tunnel. It was once part of the Galway to

---

137 Wilkins, 'Defence Prepared', pp. 42–6.

Clifden railway line, the first section of which opened on New Year's Day 1895. This was a Midland Great Western Railway Company project, and the line – which was over 48 miles in length and cost £5,000 per mile to construct – was fully completed on 1 July 1895. There were seven stations along the route, situated about seven or eight miles apart, and twenty-eight main bridges, beginning at Forster Street.[138]

At Bohermore a huge tunnel was constructed beneath the road, built of limestone and red bricks. There were a number of manholes or recesses located along the interior of the tunnel, should anyone need to stand out of the way of a passing train. Children, and indeed some adults, sat at the top of the tunnel on either side and awaited the train – it was great fun for the children when a blast of smoke shot up from beneath them as the train emerged from the tunnel. In those days wristwatches were scarce, but even children knew the time once the train reached the tunnel, as it was rarely late. The tunnel was always a favourite play area for them and they were often referred to as the 'railway children'.

Over the years there was only one incident, which occurred during the 1920s when some boys decided to tie a rope around a large stone and pull it up over the centre of the tunnel mouth. This proved extremely difficult, as the stone was much heavier than they thought. When they had the stone halfway up, the sound of the oncoming train frightened them, and although they pulled with all of their might, it was too late. The train arrived and crashed into the stone. The boys were terrified and fled as the train screeched

138 Semple, *Reflections on Lough Corrib*, pp. 161–3.

to a stop some distance along the railway line. A slightly injured and shocked driver emerged to examine the damage and investigate what had happened.

There were three boys involved in the incident, and one of them was actually the son of the train driver. However, another boy was blamed, and although he knew who was involved, he never betrayed the others and simply accepted the punishment. One of the boys involved later became an Augustinian priest and worked in the foreign missions in Nigeria for many years. One night he told the story of the railway children to some friends and his bishop, who was visiting the settlement. They were all amused, but the bishop advised him to make a public confession about the incident, as an innocent boy had been blamed, and regardless of time and distance the record should be corrected. A short time later, the story of the railway children appeared in the *Far East* magazine.[139]

Once the train passed through the tunnel at Bohermore, it had to cross two bridges in close proximity to each other, one over the Headford road and the other over the Dyke road. The River Corrib was spanned at the Waterside by a large viaduct, comprising three 150-foot iron spans supported by limestone columns.[140] For many years the railway carried the rich and famous to Connemara, where they enjoyed fishing, shooting and, of course, the scenery. The railway children always waved at the passengers and it

---

139 W. Henry, 'The Railway Children', *St Patrick's Parish Magazine* 2010, pp. 12–13.

140 Semple, *Reflections on Lough Corrib*, pp. 161–3.

was a bonus when the wave was returned. Sometimes they imagined that they were 'Indians', and the 'Iron Horse' only passed through their land because they allowed it to do so.

The railway was the beginning of a long journey across the world for many young people. It also carried young men off to the Great War. During the Irish War of Independence it sometimes carried Black and Tans, while Republicans blew up its tracks. By the 1930s the line was declared uneconomical, as the service was a heavy drain on company resources. The railway line was also in need of repairs and there was no guarantee that the huge cost involved could ever be recuperated. It closed on 27 April 1935 as the last train pulled out from Clifden. The whistle was blown several times as it left the station. Along the route people gathered to wave farewell to the train as it made its final journey to Galway Station.[141] At the old railway tunnel a huge crowd gathered to bid farewell to the train as it passed beneath them for the last time. It was the end of an era in many ways, particularly for the railway children, as they would never have the same fun again. The train saluted its faithful supporters with a puff of smoke and a blast of its whistle for the last time.

Over time new generations of railway children emerged and spent many long hours playing various games in the inky darkness of the old tunnel. Once development began in the area, the tunnel was lost to the children. Many people have no idea of its existence, but it remains today, hidden away beneath the road, a relic of another time.

---

141 K. Villiers-Tuthill, *Beyond the Twelve Bens* (Kathleen Villiers-Tuthill, 1990), pp. 99, 101, 112, 114.

Prospect Hill Reservoirs

H idden behind St Bridget's Terrace on Prospect Hill are the remains of a blocked doorway and fine cut-stone alcove inserted into the old railway wall. People wondered about them for years, some believing that they were part of an ancient church. In fact, they are all that remains of Galway's first reservoirs, the Prospect Hill reservoirs, which supplied Galway city with running water for the first time in 1868. The water was pumped up from the River Corrib to fill the two reservoirs, thus allowing gravity to supply water to the town below.[142] The road that runs behind the terrace was appropriately known as Pump Lane. Before the construction of the reservoirs, deep wells located within the city provided water to the population. The wells were located in convenient parts of the town. They were protected by government statute to ensure a clean and safe water supply, which lasted until at least the eighteenth century, when sanitary conditions began to deteriorate. Water was also drawn from the River Corrib, a practice that dated from the earliest times.[143] By the mid-nineteenth century a new water supply was required and the obvious choice was Prospect Hill, given its location on high ground

---

142 P. O'Dowd, *St Bridget's Terrace 1912–1987* (St Bridget's Terrace Residents Association, 1987), p. 10.

143 J. P. Murray, *Galway: A Medico-Social History* (Galway: Kenny's Bookshop & Art Gallery, 1994), p. 25.

overlooking the town. While this was an ideal position, the reservoirs were never a great success, as they had regular leakage problems, which caused flooding on the site from time to time. However, it took some forty years for the local authorities to act and decide to close the reservoirs. A short time later they were demolished, leaving the site free.[144]

The Prospect Hill reservoirs were replaced by the then new waterworks at Terryland.[145] The force of water from the River Corrib flowing through the Terryland River drove two turbines. In 1928 a single semi-diesel engine was installed to supplement the turbines and in 1934 the waterworks was electrified via the newly constructed Shannon Hydro-Electricity Scheme. The site of the old reservoirs on Prospect Hill is now occupied by St Bridget's Terrace, which opened in 1912.

Monster Meeting
at the Sliding Rock

The Sliding Rock is located almost at the centre of the Shantalla housing estate. Local folklore indicates that it was used as a mass rock during penal times. A large cross was later erected on top of the rock and today it is the focal point of

---

144 O'Dowd, *St Bridget's Terrace*, p. 10.
145 'Sanitation and Water Supply', *Galway Advertiser*, 5 October 1995.

a small park where children play. Not many people are aware of the fact that on 25 June 1843 the Sliding Rock became the scene for one of Daniel O'Connell's famous 'Monster Meetings', agitating for the repeal of the Act of Union, which was introduced by the British government of William Pitt the Younger on 1 January 1801. This Act dissolved the Irish parliament in Dublin, leaving the parliament at Westminster to legislate for both Ireland and England. It was supposed to solve all the problems of Ireland and was described as a marriage between the two countries. At first it seemed that Ireland had much to gain from this union: much-needed investment and free trade between both countries was promised, as was an end to discrimination by England against Irish industry, which had been common practice at the time. It was also believed that Catholic Emancipation, which would be beneficial to three-quarters of the population of Ireland, would follow in the wake of the Act. However, the harsh reality was very different, and within a short time contemporaries were describing the 'marriage' as a brutal rape. Free trade enabled England to use Ireland as a market for surplus goods and the promised investment did not materialise. Unemployment became widespread as Irish industry collapsed under direct administration. Catholic Emancipation was not granted until 1829 and then only after a long and desperate struggle. The repeal of the union became the most important objective for the Irish peasantry; in the years leading up to the Great Famine campaigns against the Act gathered momentum. This was the reason for O'Connell's visit to Galway. The following is a description of this historic event, an important part of Ireland's social and political history.

On the morning of O'Connell's visit, all the trade guilds of Galway assembled in the town. They took their places in the procession travelling to Oranmore to greet the 'Liberator' when he arrived at 2.00 p.m. that day. There was a great air of excitement as thousands gathered for the march. The appearance of the trade guilds, with their magnificent banners and insignias, was splendid. At the head of the momentous gathering was the Temperance Band, dressed in uniforms of dark green embroidered jackets and blue trousers with white seams. Their peaked caps were circled with silver bands. The fishermen then lined up, their banners and hats decorated with ribbons. While most of them were dressed in white flannel jackets, some were wearing blue. The guild of tailors, with their coat of arms displaying the beheading of St John the Baptist and the motto 'Union is Strength', followed them. Their beautifully decorated banner displaying trees, symbols of the Garden of Eden, and an entwined serpent with the forbidden fruit in its mouth was borne on a carriage drawn by four horses.

The millers were next: this 'respectable body of men' carried their decorated standard. The tobacco spinners then took their place, displaying their image of Sir Walter Raleigh being presented with a narcotic weed by an American Indian. The motto on this banner read: 'We are a long time in chains and now we must be free, Liberator of Ireland there's a welcome here for thee.' The guild of bakers followed, dressed appropriately in their respective coloured silk scarves and jackets. The stonecutters produced a magnificent green silk banner with Moses receiving the Ten Commandments on the tablets of stone. This was produced in oil, was of the highest quality and was accompanied by the motto: 'Love to God and Love to Man'. The reverse side contained the five orders of architecture and the arms of the trade, over which their motto – 'May God enable us to assist each other' – was displayed. A second banner and flag were supported by two apprentices in 'handsome uniform'. The rope makers were next, with their standard displaying the emblems of the trade and surmounted at the top with the inscription: 'O'Connell and justice to Ireland', and beneath this: 'May trade flourish'. On the reverse the Galway Ark and Rope Makers were proudly displayed at work with a motto declaring: 'Equality and no ascendancy'.

The Printers' Guild of *The Galway Vindicator* had a press placed in a boat, which was mounted on a carriage drawn by four horses. The banner was embroidered with silver stars and the inscription, in silver letters, called for 'The Constitutional Liberty of the Press'. Mounted at the other end of the carriage was a large white satin flag embroidered with gold shamrocks and the inscription: 'Old Ireland – Letter Press Printers'. The press itself was beautifully ornamented with flowers, evergreens and a white satin flag.

The guilds of butchery, shoemakers, ship carpenters, coopers and cabinet makers all followed in their respective uniforms, shouldering banners and proudly displaying mottos such as 'Division is Weakness', 'Repeal, Repeal' and 'The Son of Freedom Burnt through the Clouds of Corruption'. The sailors, painters and smiths, all well represented, were out in colourful force. The weavers' guild was at the rear of the enormous procession as it made its way towards Oranmore. Their banner displayed a lion and lioness with the motto: 'Repeal of the Union Irish Manufacturers'.

At Merlin Park the procession was met by trade guilds from County Clare. When it reached Oranmore it was met by bands from Gort and Loughrea who played a salute to the various guilds as they passed.

It was about 4.30 p.m. before Daniel O'Connell arrived. Many leading politicians and gentlemen, including Lord Ffrench, Sir Valentine Blake, MP, Dr Browne, the bishop of Galway, Robert Dillon Browne, MP, Michael Blake of Frenchfort and James Blake of Waterdale accompanied him. The procession enthusiastically re-formed and moved off towards Galway city and the Sliding Rock, where a huge stage had been erected for the occasion. It was an amazing sight, with O'Connell in his carriage, his entourage and bands leading the way, together with 'innumerable cars and a whole line of equestrians'. They were followed by at least 500,000 people: an enormous gathering. One report stated, 'the patriotic union of countrymen, for more than thirty miles distant, came under a scorching sun to prove their love of fatherland and freedom'.

The town was also adorned with banners and flags, many of them in the Irish language and even more in English, all of them more or less making the same demands: 'Ireland for the Irish'. At Eyre Square a pavilion had been set up for a public dinner that was planned for later that evening. It bore the British ensign and was supported on either side by flags emblazoned with the harp and the Irish cry 'Repeal'. As the colossal cortège passed through the streets every window was 'crowded with the patriotic people waving handkerchiefs, green scarves and shawls in salutation to the Liberator'.

The imposing procession reached the centre of the town. There was no standing room available on the footpaths and people simply were caught up in the march to Shantalla. The bands continued to play and their rendition of the 'Conquering Hero' inspired the hearts of people with overpowering patriotism. When the cortège reached the Shambles Barracks near Bridge Street each band played 'God Save the Queen' as it passed, a sentiment cheered with the utmost enthusiasm. The procession proceeded to the Sliding Rock, located at that time on the lands of Thomas Bodkin, who had given over his fields for the meeting. It was 7.00 p.m. when it reached the venue and the dignitaries mounted the platform to the sound of the bands. When the music stopped Lord Ffrench moved to the centre of the stage to address the immense gathering and the crowd began cheering loudly. He thanked and welcomed all present and spoke words of encouragement about the future. Sir Valentine Blake then addressed the masses and was followed in turn by the other speakers. All of them condemned the Act of Union and called for repeal in the strongest possible terms. Finally, the Liberator was presented to the crowd.

As soon as he spoke the assembly began cheering and this continued for several minutes. When at last silence fell over the masses, Daniel O'Connell told them that he was in no doubt that the Act must be repealed; that no power on earth could prevent the people from achieving this objective. He said that he had already asked two million of the crowd's fellow countrymen if they would have repeal and they had all 'answered in the affirmative'. O'Connell called out to the Galway people, asking if they wanted repeal with the same determination. The reply was swift and loud as the people began shouting, almost hysterically, 'We would die for it!' He assured them that death was not the answer, adding that it would be far better to have 'one living patriot than a hundred dead ones', which urged the masses to call out 'Hear, hear' in support. O'Connell then informed the crowd that the purpose of his visit was to offer a challenge, but also he denounced anything that would lead to violence and bloodshed. The challenge, he said, was to historians, to point out that in the history of the world never had there been 'so pure and holy a cause'. The multitude cheered louder.

As the applauding subsided, O'Connell called out again, saying that he wanted to 'prevent domination by the Saxon and the Alien'. There was uproar. O'Connell, playing to the crowd, shouted out, 'Ireland belongs to the Irish!' He added that it was impossible to overrate the importance of the cause, and he was delighted with the repeal movement to date. Ireland, he said, was the most beautiful land the sun had ever shone upon, 'her bays were safe and capacious and her rivers afforded means for trade and commerce unequalled by any other nation'. Yes, this country was worth struggling for, he called out, adding even Cromwell, when pursuing his march of death and devastation, upon viewing the beauty and fertility of the land, exclaimed, 'Is not this a country worth fighting for?' This sent the gathering into a frenzy of applause and cheering.

Moments later O'Connell informed the people that newspaper reports had stated that Tory politicians, the Duke of Wellington and Robert Peel had announced 'a falsehood of a treasonable nature' in the House of Commons by saying that the Queen was against the repeal of the union. There was an immediate response as people began shouting that this was a lie. He added that the government laughed at the idea of civil war in Ireland, but, if they were attacked, 'woe be to him who assailed them'. Peel, it seemed, had done much damage to the repeal movement and O'Connell said that he had 'grown thin in consequence of it, as if he had fasted' for another Lent. Upon hearing this statement, the gathering broke out in great laughter. O'Connell was on excellent form. 'The Duke of Wellington, Sir Robert Peel and Lord Stanley [Edward Smith-Stanley, 14th Earl of Derby]', he said, 'could think of nothing better for Ireland than to arrest old women who sang ballads in the street.' More laughter.

After the crowd had settled again, O'Connell said Sir James Graham, another British statesman, had the 'atrocious audacity' to say that the Catholic prelates, clergy, nobility and laity of Ireland were guilty of perjury. The laughter of the crowd turned to groans. He went on to speak about the granting of Catholic Emancipation. 'Thank you for nothing!' he shouted, adding, 'They granted it because they could not help it.' Speaking of the Protestant church and its appointment of bishops, he stated that he did not care how many they appointed, provided their own parishioners funded them, rather than forcing Catholics to finance them 'while our poor have either to starve or go into prison'.

O'Connell then returned to the subject of repeal and promised the crowd that if it were successful hospitals would be erected to maintain the poor in comfort, every man would own a house and 'no man would be without a vote, unless a blackguard, or a fellow who was too ugly to get an honest girl to marry him'. The huge gathering erupted into laughter again. When this subsided, O'Connell went off on a more serious note on the subject of absentee landlords. These people, he said, were taking £9 million annually out of Ireland, but repeal would put an end to that. He also spoke of evictions and of landlords taking advantage of their positions when it came to education, compelling Catholic children to attend Protestant schools to be educated in their politics and discourage repeal. Was anything, he asked, more atrocious than the corruption of the mind?

However, O'Connell also gave credit to kind-hearted landlords. He told them that repeal would also support tenants who worked on improving their homes and would request landlords to compensate people for all repairs and improvements carried out. He said that the national debt of Ireland could be reduced and taxation removed, or at least be greatly reduced. If this was achieved, he called out, tea, sugar, tobacco and everything that gave comfort to the poor would be cheaper.

Speaking of the national debt of both Ireland and England, he said, 'John Bull was anxious to make a bargain with us and thus he will say, "Now, Paddy, you owe 20 millions of national debt, and I'll pay half of that for you. I am much obliged to you says poor Paddy, but then you will have to pay half mine, 446 millions."' O'Connell's sarcasm and wit lifted the people again. But he then warned, 'the time was coming fast when John Bull would have to pay his own debts', and asked, 'is there a man among you who would not be willing to undergo toil, fatigue, and even the peril of death, if necessary to achieve repeal?' The crowd responded with great enthusiasm and support, some again shouting that they would die for it. O'Connell, however, stressed that he did not want such extremes: all he required from the people was to register as members of the Repeal Association. This, he said, would cost them a farthing per week, a penny per month or a shilling annually. They would then be on the road to repeal.

Before finishing O'Connell said that 'Liberty and prosperity would be the result' for those following his path. If the people chose to abandon him, he continued, there was nothing he could do about that, but he added that for his part he would never abandon Ireland. After his death, people would say, 'Here lies the man who repealed the atrocious Union.' At this there were was an eruption of immense cheering that echoed across the countryside and lasted for several minutes.

It was 9.00 p.m. by the time the 'monster meeting' finished. The people immediately formed into processional ranks again and began the journey back towards the town to the sounds of the bands leading them.

A banquet took place the following evening and again the guilds of trade and bands marched through the town, no doubt leaving the Liberator with fond and unforgettable memories of his visit to Galway.[146]

---

146 'Magnificent Repeal Demonstration in Galway', *The Galway Vindicator*, 28 June 1843.

Milestones at Roscam

There are a number of discarded milestones lying along the headland and beach at Roscam. A local woman discovered them some years ago and pointed them out to historian Peadar O'Dowd. He subsequently documented and later published the details in an article on milestones in the *Galway Archaeological and Historical Journal*.

Milestones were important road markers to weary travellers in centuries past as they indicated the miles left to travel before reaching one's destination. There are many examples surviving throughout County Galway and they are wonderful reminders of our past. Some are very basic, with simply the mile marked, but others also have destinations carved on to them. There are also some unusual ones with delightful little carvings, such as the one at Annagh Cross, which has a small hand carved into it pointing in the direction of the destination.[147]

Following the discovery at Roscam, Jacqueline O'Brien, her children David and Gavin and two friends, Gavin Duffy and Brian Shields, made a thorough search of the seafront at Roscam. Two expeditions were organised in May 2001 and the hunt commenced, covering some very rough terrain.

---

147 P. O'Dowd, 'On Roads and Milestones in County Galway', *Journal of the Galway Archaeological & Historical Society*, vol. 53, 2001, pp. 105–7, 116.

The group discovered eleven additional milestones. It is not known where these milestones were originally located or how they found their way to Roscam. It has been suggested that this cluster of important roadside monuments could possibly have been victims of road development sometime over the past seventy years. There is also some confusion about these particular examples as it has also been suggested that these finds are tide stones and have nothing to do with public travel. Nevertheless, they are an important find regardless of their purpose and are a valuable part of our heritage.[148]

A Scientific Genius

Richard Kirwan, chemist and scientist, was born at Cloughballymore, County Galway, in 1733. He lived with his parents until he was eight years old and then went to live with relations, the French family from the same area. It was through reading science books in his uncle's library that he developed an interest in chemistry. He later attended the Erasmus Smith School in Galway. In 1754 he travelled to France, where he entered a Jesuit novitiate.

Kirwan returned to Galway the following year and went to live at Cregg Castle, which he had inherited from

---

148 W. Henry, 'Mile Stones at Roscam', *St Patrick's Parish Magazine* 2001.

his brother who had been killed in a duel. He became a Protestant and studied law at Trinity College Dublin. Although called to the Irish bar, he declined, as he wanted to pursue science and chemistry. In 1757 Kirwan married Anne Blake of Menlo Castle, where the couple lived for several years. He built up a substantial library and when he began conducting experiments he had one of the rooms at the castle specially renovated for this purpose. It was there that Kirwan spent many long hours, working late into the night, much to the distaste of his mother-in-law. His dedication to science is evident from a comment she once made regarding his work, saying that she 'never intended her daughter to be the wife of a monk'. Anne died in 1765.

Kirwan remained in Galway until 1777 and then travelled to London. It was during this period that his reputation as a scientist grew to such a degree that he was recognised throughout Europe and the United States. He had a good command of European languages, which helped him correspond with other leading men of science in Europe.[149]

In 1780 he was elected as a fellow of the Royal Society and two years later was awarded the Copley medal (for outstanding achievements in research) for his substantial contribution to analytical chemistry. While Kirwan seems to have enjoyed his time and success abroad, he returned to Ireland in 1787. He set up home in Dublin and was equally well respected in the Irish capital, as is evident from his election to the presidency of the Royal Irish Academy a relatively short time later.

---

149 'Old Galway', *Galway Advertiser*, 31 January 1985.

Kirwan published many papers and books, some of which caused controversy among his peers. In particular, he was one of the last scientists to support the theory of the existence of a fire-like element called 'phlogiston', supposedly released during combustion. His *Elements of Mineralogy* was published in 1784 and was the first book of its kind to be made available in the English language.[150] His contribution to agriculture was contained in a paper he published on various manures, a work that was acknowledged as being of great significance in the history of agriculture. He is believed to have been the first to pursue a scientific study of meteorology, which resulted in many farmers consulting with him before sowing crops.[151] He was also an excellent geologist and it was through his efforts that the museum of the Royal Dublin Society bought a rich collection of minerals known as the Leskean Cabinet.

Kirwan had two daughters, but very little is known of them. He continued to live in Dublin, where he died on 21 June 1812. He is buried in St George's Churchyard, Lower Temple Street, Dublin.[152]

150 'Richard Kirwan (Chemist, Mineralogist, Meteorologist and Geologist)', http://irishscientists.tripod.com/scientists/RICHARD. HTM (May 2010).

151 'Old Galway', *Galway Advertiser*, 31 January 1985.

152 'Kirwan, Richard (1733–1812)' in H. Maher, *Galway Authors* (Galway: Galway County Libraries, 1976), pp. 58–9.

Prince of Preachers

Father Tom Burke, the great lecturer and preacher of the nineteenth century, was born on 8 September 1830 in Galway. He received his early education at the Monastery School in Lombard Street and it was there that Brother Paul O'Connor, founder of the Patrician Brothers in Galway, sowed the seeds of Burke's future greatness. At seventeen he entered the Dominican Order and studied in Rome and Perugia.[153] Four years later he was transferred to Woodchester in Gloucestershire to take charge of a newly appointed novitiate. In 1855 Burke returned to Ireland where he was appointed superintendent of a new novitiate in Tallaght, Dublin, and became spiritual director to the students. In 1867 he delivered an oration over the tomb of Daniel O'Connell in Glasnevin Cemetery, Dublin, before a crowd of 50,000 people. A short time later he found himself in Rome as prior of San Clemente. He attended the Vatican Council of 1870 as theologian to Dr J. P. Leahy, Bishop of Dromore.

On 12 October 1871 Burke sailed from Liverpool to New York to visit the American Dominican houses and while there received many invitations to preach and lecture. Thus began his great preaching crusade: Pope Pius XI awarded him the title 'Prince of Preachers'. There are in existence some eighteen letters from American bishops praising Fr

---

153 'Thomas Nicholas Burke (1830–1883)', *Galway: Official Guide to City and County*, 1986, p. 61.

Burke's wonderful work while in the United States. Day after day, his lectures and sermons were delivered with an eloquence and power that seemed supernatural. It was said that he electrified his congregation with spontaneous outbursts of expressiveness. He became immensely popular and raised large sums of money in just eighteen months through his sermons and speeches.

Following his American tour, Burke returned to Galway where his old teacher, Paul O'Connor, greeted him with an address of welcome at the school in Lombard Street. A short time later he travelled to Dublin and was assigned to Tallaght Priory, where he spent the last ten years of his life. By the early 1880s he was experiencing health problems and made frequent visits to Rome, where he hoped the warm climate would improve his rapidly deteriorating health. Although extremely ill, Fr Burke delivered his last sermon on 22 June 1883. According to a reporter of *The Freeman's Journal*, he held the congregation spellbound with the eloquence of his tongue at this charity sermon to raise money for 5,000 starving children in Donegal.

On 2 July 1883 the 'Prince of Preachers' died in Tallaght. He was laid to rest in the church, which has since been dedicated to his memory.[154] In 1948 a limestone statue of the famous preacher was unveiled at Fr Burke Road in Galway, which was also named in his honour. The sculptor was Seán Kavanagh from Cork.[155]

---

154 Ó hEideain, *Dominicans in Galway*, pp. 91–5.

155 P. O'Dowd, *Down by the Claddagh* (Galway: Kenny's Bookshop and Art Galleries, 1993), pp. 130–1.

Cooper's Cave

There is a cave located in the fields behind Glenburren Park housing estate, close to the Font roundabout on the Tuam road. It was known locally as Cooper's Cave. Children from all over the city were always warned to stay away from it for fear of being lost or trapped in its chambers. However, these warnings were mostly ignored – the spirit of adventure always prevailed. The hope of finding a highwayman's stolen treasure was also a reason to take little notice of the warnings. According to legend, the cave takes its name from a highwayman named Cooper who was supposed to have used it as his hideout. Others say that he hid his booty in the cave, but nothing has ever been found there. There is no direct evidence to link the cave to Cooper, just tradition.

The cave was once located in the countryside, but the massive spread of urban development in Galway has now positioned it within the confines of the city. It seems that with the introduction of television during the 1960s came the loss of children's adventurous spirit, thus Cooper's Cave was all but forgotten. Some years ago people who moved into new housing close by began to explore their surroundings and upon finding the cave believed that they had made a new discovery![156]

---

156   W. Henry, 'Cooper's Cave', *St Patrick's Parish Magazine* 2010, p. 6.

The Forgotten Land League Campaigner

Thomas Ashe was a leading Galway campaigner in the Irish Land League movement. He is now almost forgotten in the town where he devoted much of his life to trying to secure a better standard of living for the people.

Ashe was born in 1854 in Quay Street. As a young man, he became one of the most prominent political figures in Galway. During the late nineteenth century he was involved with Charles Stewart Parnell and the Irish Parliamentary Party. He also served as an independent member of the town commissioners and the board of guardians. His activities were not confined to the Land League or Galway – he was also actively involved in several nationalist movements and he served two terms in prison. However, this did not discourage or dampen his beliefs in the Irish cause.

On a social level, Ashe worked hard in having the 'Swamp' area close to the Claddagh reclaimed from the sea. This area is known today as South Park, but to the older Galwegians it is still the 'Swamp'. This important campaign provided a wonderful place of recreation for the public and continues to be developed in present times. There is also a wonderful walking area overlooking Galway Bay.

Ashe was also active in sports and was the captain of a local hurling team. By the mid-1880s, he was devoting almost all of his time to serving the public and battled tirelessly for better standards of living for the poor of the town. This work possibly contributed to his health deteriorating in a short space of time. He never married and died a relatively young man at the County Infirmary at Prospect Hill in June 1892. His funeral mass took place in the pro-cathedral and was followed by his burial in the New Cemetery, Bohermore. Four black horses drew the hearse, while the coffin was borne by members of the National League (the nationalist political party founded in October 1882 by Charles Stewart Parnell after the suppression of the Land League). Some 600 members of the league and a large representation from the various Gaelic clubs marched in procession behind the hearse. The cortège, which was one of the biggest ever seen in the city, was led by the band of the National League. Upwards of 10,000 mourners lined the route to pay their respects. The Charles Stewart Parnell National League Branch, while paying tribute to Ashe's 'sterling patriotism', stated: 'his death has created a void in the ranks of the independents of this town which will take a long time to fill'. Ashe's funeral was second in size only to that of Charles Stewart Parnell.[157]

On 11 June 1892 *The Galway Observer* reported, 'few men in Galway have taken so remarkable a part in local politics as that by Mr Ashe for this last six years ... there are few who exerted their influence with such effect as he did in carrying out whatever he took in hand'.[158]

157 'Thomas Ashe Centenary to be marked in the city', *Galway City Tribune*, 3 June 1992.
158 'Death of Thomas Ashe', *The Galway Observer*, 11 June 1892.

Thomas Ashe did not live long enough to see the fruits of the Gaelic Revival – the late-nineteenth-century renewal of interest in Irish language and culture – but he certainly played a guiding role towards a nationalist Ireland. His niece, Maggie Ann Ashe, later took a position on Galway Urban Council and was a member of the first modern Galway Corporation when it was reformed in 1937. In 1992 a centenary mass was celebrated for Thomas Ashe in the Augustinian church and was attended by the mayor and Galway Corporation and representatives of the Parnell Commemorative Committee. Following the mass, a wreath-laying ceremony took place at his grave.

A Blind Piper

Martin Reilly was born in Galway city during the mid-nineteenth century. He was blind, either from birth or from shortly afterwards, but this did not interfere with his talent for playing the pipes. Reilly lived in either Eyre Street or Suckeen, where he operated a dance hall for a number of years. There is an old stone building with a galvanised roof located in Suckeen that was possibly the place. It is widely believed that the clergy closed the hall down because it was a venue where young men and women could meet. Reilly fell into abject poverty. Piping was the only profession this talented man knew, and being blind he had no other means of supporting himself. However, with the foundation of the Gaelic League in 1893, many of the old music and dance traditions were revived and Martin Reilly, being one of the most notable pipers of his day, was invited to play in many parts of the country. He was highly respected for his talent among the leading pipers and took part in various competitions organised by the Gaelic League and others. John Potts – in later years affectionately known as 'Old Potts' – was one of the young pipers of the period. He knew Reilly well and would remove his hat when speaking of him, so great was the respect that he held for the old master.[159]

Another of Reilly's great admirers was Éamonn Ceannt, one of the founders of the Dublin Pipers' Club. Ceannt was later executed for his part in the 1916 Rebellion. In 1901, shortly after the Pipers' Club was founded in Dublin, Ceannt invited Martin Reilly to the capital to play in the annual feis. Ceannt looked after his needs and accommodation and, indeed, any time the old piper visited Dublin he would stay in Ceannt's home.[160] Reilly gave an excellent performance and his piping was noted in the Dublin newspapers. His selection, 'The Battle of Aughrim', captivated all those present and it was reported that 'the gallant old piper, throbbing with a spirit that might long to play his countrymen into battle, fired them with a stirring and strident version of the victorious march of Brian Boru.

---

159 Interview: Jack Small, 10 October 2010.

160 W. Henry, *Supreme Sacrifice: The Story of Éamonn Ceannt 1881–1916* (Cork: Mercier Press, 2005), p. 15.

He played in perfect tune and produced marvellous tones on his instrument.' Another report stated: 'The wonderful old man played the ancient airs with such a feeling of expression and profound understanding, that he simply took the house by storm.' Reilly's performances won him first prize in the piping section.[161]

Reporting on the Pipers' Club concert in February 1903, a contributor to *The Gael* stated:

> Martin Reilly is our last truly great piper. His performance of the famous 'Fox Chase' was a relic of old times. His 'Battle of Aughrim', a vividly descriptive piece of playing, is likely to be spoken of in Dublin Gaelic circles for many a long day. It is to be hoped this veteran blind piper may be given opportunities of displaying his skill during the coming year in all parts of Ireland.[162]

In 1904 Reilly played at a Gaelic League concert in the Town Hall in Galway. Among the audience was another avid admirer of his music, Douglas Hyde, who later became President of Ireland.[163]

Martin Reilly never had an easy life and this sightless man was constantly plagued by poverty and hunger. He was forced to enter the workhouse on a number of occasions to avoid starvation. Reilly's final days were spent in Gort Workhouse. There is a story that when he was lying on his deathbed the last thing he asked for was his 'beloved'

161 M. Naughton, *The History of St Francis Parish* (Mary Naughton, undated), pp. 22–3.
162 'Pipers' Club Concert', *An Piobaire*, vol. 6, no. 4, September 2010.
163 Naughton, *History of St Francis Parish*, pp. 22–3.

pipes.[164] A short time later Éamonn Ceannt wrote an article called 'The Irish Piper' in which he acknowledged Reilly:

> We have said that the great pipers are all gone. The last of them is not long dead. He was a blind man from Galway, Martin Reilly by name, who was rescued from the poorhouse by Pádraig Mac an Fhailghe and boomed by Cumann na Píobairí. He had just time to make his debut to the Gaels of Dublin and many other Irish centres when death claimed him for his own. His loss was sorely felt by many who looked forward to hearing him again. May he rest in peace, Amen.

An Infamous Landlord and Miser

Hubert George de Burgh, landlord, miser and Second Marquis of Clanricarde, was born on 30 November 1832. He was the second son of Ulick de Burgh and Harriet Canning, the daughter of George Canning, the British Prime Minister. De Burgh was educated at Harrow and it seems that he was unhappy during his time there. In 1852 he entered the diplomatic service and was attached to the legation at Turin in Italy. At that time, members of the foreign office – 'attachés' – were expected to finance themselves. The allowance Hubert received from his father was such that it rendered him close to a state of continuous poverty, and he was sometimes forced to seek a night's accommodation

---

164 Interview: Jack Small, 10 October 2010.

in a broom cupboard in his place of employment. He also tailored his own clothes, which made him a bit of an oddity among his peers.

Hubert de Burgh's father's lack of financial support was due mainly to spendthrift habits on his own part and the excessive generosity he extended to his eldest son, (Ulick) Lord Dunkellin, who later became an MP for Galway and who was well liked throughout Ireland and much favoured by his father.[165] A statue to Lord Dunkellin stood inside the main entrance to Eyre Square for many years, but was pulled down following the signing of the Anglo-Irish Treaty in 1921.[166]

In August 1867 Lord Dunkellin died and his father asked Hubert to take his brother's seat in parliament. By this time Hubert had amassed considerable wealth and property, much of it (some £250,000) gained from the death of an uncle, Charles Canning, after whom he took the name Canning. However, the money did nothing to change his miserly lifestyle. He resigned his seat in parliament in 1871 as a protest against William Gladstone's Irish Land Act, which reduced rents for tenants (Hubert himself was one of the notorious absentee landlords, who charged his tenants exorbitant rents but did not live within his property's economic region). Keeping his huge fortune intact had already become an obsession. When de Burgh's father died in 1874 he made a brief visit to Galway to attend the funeral in Portumna. However, the main reason

---

165 M. Shiel and D. Roche (eds), *A Forgotten Campaign and Aspects of the Heritage of South-East Galway* (Galway: East Galway Centenary Group, Woodford Heritage Group, 1986), p. 13.

166 'Eyre Square: Monuments and Markets', *Galway Independent*, 10 February 2010.

for his visit may have been to secure the family estate.[167] He continued to have little regard for the land or his tenants and regarded the estate as a means of earning more money to add to his already immense fortune.

Hubert de Burgh has been described as 'a tyrannical landlord with a heart of stone' and 'Ireland's meanest man'. He was refused entry to the House of Lords on a number of occasions because of his unkempt and unwashed appearance. It was said that while living in London he was pitied as he made his way home with cheap fish or vegetables wrapped in dirty newspapers. Needless to say, this compassion was from those who were unaware of his circumstances.[168] This 'walking scarecrow without crows', as he was sometimes called, ate very little and even at home his greatest extravagance was a couple of boiled eggs.[169]

By 1886 de Burgh's tenants in East Galway were being forced to pay exorbitantly high rents and when they could not meet the payments de Burgh would have them evicted.[170] The Great Famine of 1845–50 had already seen the continuous eviction of tenant farmers, and many people had found themselves in the workhouse or on an emigrant ship. This precedent, along with the high rents and evictions, led to land agitation and the foundation of the Irish National Land League.

Resistance to evictions came to a head in 1886 near

---

167 Shiel and Roche (eds), *Forgotten Campaign*, pp. 14, 15.
168 L. Bowes, 'When Ireland's Meanest Man Became M.P. for Galway', *Ireland's Own*, August 1991.
169 Shiel and Roche (eds), *Forgotten Campaign*, p. 15.
170 Bowes, 'Ireland's Meanest Man'.

Woodford, County Galway, with the so-called 'Siege of Sanders' Fort'. A number of men barricaded themselves into the house of Thomas Sanders, who was to be evicted on the orders of de Burgh because he refused to pay the excessively high rent demanded.[171] The eviction was to take place on 20 August, but the sheriff and his men did not expect the resistance they faced that evening. The barricades held and the men dropped beehives on the attackers, causing panic amongst their ranks. The eviction attempt failed and the authorities retreated after a number of hours. The following morning a larger force gathered to evict Sanders and his supporters from the house. However, this attack also failed, and the force returned to Portumna to await reinforcements. On Friday 27 August 1886, a 'small army' consisting of 700 police, two companies of troops and forty 'emergency-men' marched out from Portumna for the assault on Sanders' house. The defenders did extremely well against such overwhelming odds, using lime, boiling water, and beehives and rolling huge stones off the roof. However, the enemy's vast numbers eventually broke through with the support of the Crowbar Brigade and twenty-two defenders were arrested.

Although the siege ended successfully for the authorities, it captured the imagination of the men involved in the land war. When the prisoners were released they returned to a heroes' welcome and witnessed the burning of effigies of de Burgh.[172]

---

171   Henry, *Supreme Sacrifice*, p. 3.
172   T. Feeney and A. Ó Máille, 'The Siege of Sander's Fort' in Roche and Shiel (eds), *Forgotten Campaign*, pp. 16, 22–3, 25.

No lessons were learned by de Burgh following the Woodford evictions. He continued to extract excessive rents from his tenants. He also resisted any attempts by the government to support tenant farmers. In fact, the only speech he made in the House of Lords was to reject and denounce an attempt by the government to implement an Evicted Tenants Bill in 1907. It was reported that his speech was met with 'chilling silence' from the house. Two years later the government endowed the Congested Districts Board with the power of compulsory land acquisition. The board decided to use its powers against de Burgh through the courts. This was a difficult task, but finally, on 29 July 1915, the compulsory purchase of his estate was settled for £238,221. Hubert de Burgh died in April 1916, leaving behind an immense fortune and property valued at £2,500,000. He was buried in London without much pomp or ceremony.

It is not surprising that people remembered him as a 'solitary, smelly, absurd figure, dressed in second-hand clothes bought in some flea-market'. Another report stated, 'He was a millionaire, a miser, a recluse and a connoisseur of objets d'art and no man did more to injure the unionist cause in Ireland.'[173] One wonders if the financial difficulties he experienced as a young man in Italy had made him the despicable character who most people avoided.

Hubert de Burgh was the last of the Clanricardes and his death signalled the end of one of the greatest Anglo-Norman families of Ireland.

---

173   *Ibid.*, pp. 13, 16–17.

William from Galway

❧⟡❧

There is a long tradition in Galway of Christopher Columbus having visited the town. Some old tales mention that while on his voyage of discovery in 1492 he stopped in Galway and picked up an experienced seaman named William Penrice, who knew of 'land beyond the sea'. The story also relates how this William from Galway was the first European to set foot on American shores, even though St Brendan the Navigator is also credited with having reached the shores of the New World from Galway hundreds of years earlier. Indeed, there were widespread stories of earlier voyages to the west at that time, and legends of lost islands and a lost continent which would have given Columbus confidence in his theory of there being land to the west.[174]

William from Galway makes a great story, particularly for visiting Americans, and over the years local people and indeed some historical guides have exploited it. As with all great legends, there is an element of truth once the myth is cleared away. In 1992 the late Professor of History, T. P. O'Neill, gave a lecture to the Old Galway Society based on his extensive research on the voyages of Christopher Columbus. During the lecture he mentioned a story of Columbus having visited Galway some years before 1492.

---

174 N. Canny, 'Remembering Columbus 1492–1992', *Journal of the Galway Archaeological & Historical Society*, vol. 44, 1992, pp. 4, 6.

During his research, Professor O'Neill came across what he described as 'tangible and hard evidence' of the voyager's visit to Galway: some writing in the margin of a book entitled the *Wonders of the World*, which was printed in 1477. The book in which Columbus mentioned his experiences in Galway was written by Aeneas Silvius Piccolomini, later Pope Pius II, and it is still preserved in Seville. The fact that Columbus thought it important enough to record and later use as evidence while making a case to raise finance for his voyage of discovery, gives an air of reality to the story.[175]

The following comment was written in Latin by Columbus himself, and translates as: 'We ourselves saw in Galway, Ireland, in two pieces of wood, a man and his wife of extraordinary visage.' There have been a number of theories put forward regarding what Columbus actually witnessed while in Galway. Some say that it was the bodies of two First Nation people (from what is now Canada) washed up on the western shoreline, or two carved effigies of these people.[176]

Another version of the story records: 'Men of Cathay have come towards the west. Of this we have seen many signs. And especially in Galway in Ireland, a man and a woman, of extraordinary appearance, have come to land on two tree trunks.' It has been suggested that the bodies of two Inuit in a timber kayak were carried southwards from Canada. Their oriental appearance may have convinced Columbus that these people were from the east.

---

175 'A Note in the Margin', *Galway Advertiser*, 2 November 1992.

176 T. P. O'Neill, 'Christopher Columbus', lecture to the Old Galway Society, 12 October 1992.

It is difficult to separate fact from fiction after 500 years. Columbus quite possibly did visit Galway, but the old tale that William from Galway was picked up by him there in 1492 belongs in the realms of legend. A more credible story is that William joined the crew of the 100-ton flagship *Santa Maria* before leaving Spain in August of that year. The logbook of the *Santa Maria* records an Irishman, Guillermo Ires, among the crew members – he was known as William from Galway. Some sources indicate that he had been released from a Spanish prison along with an Englishman to sail with Columbus. Others believe that he just happened to be in the port of Palos when Columbus was assembling his crew. While there is much speculation regarding William being in Spain, this would not be unusual given the important commercial links between Spanish ports and Galway during this period. Two other ships also set sail with the *Santa Maria* that day: the *Nina* and the *Pinta*.[177]

The reason for the voyage was to find a westward route to China or India because the overland road from the Mediterranean to the east had been cut off following the fall of Constantinople to the Turks in 1453. This destroyed the trade in spices for the merchants of Genoa. Before setting out Columbus had studied as many books as possible and listened to stories from old seamen that indicated that there was land beyond the Atlantic. What he did not anticipate was a huge continent.[178]

After almost ten years of preparation Columbus set sail

---

177 'Old Galway', *Galway Advertiser*, 31 January 1985.
178 O'Neill, 'Note in the Margin'.

from Palos on 3 August 1492, having gained the support of King Ferdinand and Queen Isabella of Spain. Columbus recorded in his journal that there was a dog on board, something his son Ferdinand also described in a book. It is believed that William took an Irish wolfhound on his journey to the new world. This would not have been so unusual given that there was an export trade in these animals too.

The ships sailed westwards and as the weeks passed concern amongst the crews of the three vessels increased. There were threats of mutiny as the sailors became increasingly apprehensive because they were so long at sea without sighting land.[179] Eventually, on 12 October 1492, a sailor on the *Pinta* sighted land: this was probably Watling Island in the Bahamas, which Columbus named San Salvador.

An Italian monk, writing in the seventeenth century, recorded that when the *Santa Maria* dropped its anchor a longboat set out from the ship. As it came close to land, an Irishman from Galway named Patrick McGuire jumped out of the boat ahead of the others in a bid to haul it ashore. However, this man is not mentioned in any of the logbooks. Who was the Irishman? Some speculate that the monk may have been mistakenly identified William from Galway as Patrick.[180]

Once ashore the Spaniards were delighted to see friendly and inquisitive natives, who were wearing gold nose rings.

179 R. Owen, *Great Explorers* (London: Peerage, 1979), pp. 51–2.
180 'Old Galway'.

The voyagers were unsure of their exact location, believing that they should have landed in Japan. They soon set sail again and began to explore other islands in the area, and on 28 October 1492 they reached the coast of Cuba. They then sailed to another island – Haiti – which Columbus named La Isla Española (in his writings Latinised to Hispaniola).[181] Upon arrival he found the king and his people friendly, so he was not overly concerned about safety. Nevertheless, he had a fort built there and named it La Navidad (Christmas) after the day of its foundation.

The *Pinta* had earlier separated from the other two ships and had now been missing for some weeks. Columbus suspected that its captain, Martin Alonzo Pinzon, was returning to Spain to seek all the glory for himself. Columbus decided to follow but asked for volunteers to remain behind while he returned to Spain to inform the king and queen of the discovery. He told those staying behind that his plan was to come back to the island with a larger fleet and relieve them so they could return home. Before leaving he cautioned his men and told them to respect the local king and his chiefs and avoid anything that might disturb the friendly relations he had established with the inhabitants.

It seems that William from Galway was among the men who volunteered to stay in the New World. The *Santa Maria* was wrecked, having struck a coral reef, so the *Nina* had to be serviced for the homeward journey. The returning party set sail on 4 January 1493. The following is a description of

---

181   Owen, *Great Explorers*, pp. 51–2.

their departure as visualised by the Italian monk (Allard is reputed to be the Englishman who enlisted with William from Galway):

> Among the little crowd on shore who watched the *Nina* growing smaller in the distance are our old friends Allard and William from Galway, tired of the crazy confinement of a ship and anxious for shore adventures. They have their fill of them as it happens; for the settlers a sudden cloud of blood and darkness. But death waits Allard and William from Galway in the sunshine and silence of Espanola.[182]

On 1 March 1493 Columbus landed at Palos, the port from which he had set out on his epic voyage. The following November when he returned as promised to La Navidad he learned of the tragic fate that had befallen the men he left behind. It is not known what exactly happened to those who remained, but apparently after he left the island Columbus' sailors took advantage of the native hospitality. Violence descended on the little colony, resulting in the deaths of all the Europeans, including William from Galway.

Christopher Columbus made three other voyages to the New World before dying in 1506.[183] When one looks out across Galway Bay today and thinks of the millions of Irish men, women and children who have sought a better life 'beyond the Atlantic', one cannot help but wonder about William from Galway, possibly the first Irishman to set foot in the New World.

---

182 'Old Galway'.
183 Owen, *Great Explorers*, pp. 51–2.

Captain Martin Kirwan:
Hero of the Franco-Prussian War

O n 13 July 1870 the French government, under Prime Minister Emile Ollivier, ordered the general mobilisation of its armies in preparation for a war against Prussia. The conflict was a culmination of years of tension between the two nations, which came to a head over the issue of a Hohenzollern – a noble family and royal dynasty – candidate being chosen by the Prussians to fill the Spanish throne, vacated in 1868 by Isabella II. A document, the Ems Dispatch, was also made public, which heightened alleged insults between the Prussian king and the French ambassador, and this inflamed public opinion on both sides.

However, the French mobilisation was chaotic and they also underestimated the Prussians, who had already defeated the Austrians in the Austro-Prussian War. The Prussians were the rising military force in Europe, having gained much experience over the previous ten years.[184]

Very little is recorded of the Irish involvement in this war, but after hostilities broke out, some 300 volunteers travelled from Ireland intending to support France by attending to the ambulance wagons. However, only 100 of them were accepted, which left the remainder with little option but to

---

184 M. Glover, *Warfare from Waterloo to Mons* (London: Cassell 1980), pp. 134–5.

return home. Those who chose to remain in France, being young, adventurous and full of fighting spirit, decided to volunteer for service in the French army and came to the attention of Lieutenant Martin Waters Kirwan from Galway, an ex-officer in the Glamorganshire Regiment.

When war had broken out, Kirwan had immediately sailed for France with the intention of forming the nucleus of a Franco-Irish regiment. He was still a young man, in his twenties, and keen to pursue his profession as a soldier. Kirwan had a strong desire to gain experience of actual combat and was sympathetic towards the French cause. He had applied to the British military authorities for leave to serve with the French army, but this had been refused, so he resigned. Upon arrival in France, Kirwan was offered command of the Irishmen who had enlisted in the French army and was given the rank of captain.

The majority of the Irish people at that time were eager to support the French and a committee was set up in Dublin to promote the cause and more volunteers made their way to France. They increased Captain Kirwan's company, building it into a regiment. There were even hopes of swelling its numbers to form a strong Irish brigade. The Foreign Enlistment Act presented some legal difficulties at first, as the French government had to sanction the enlistment of foreign nationals, but these were eventually overcome. While thousands of men throughout Ireland put their names forward to the Dublin committee, there were additional administration delays, which, coupled with the early termination of the war, rendered their service unnecessary.

Nevertheless, Kirwan and his company, who had been in France almost from the beginning, were accepted as a unit of the French army on 16 October 1870. They served from that date until the last shot of the war was fired in February of the following year. Kirwan's modest little company, which numbered exactly 100 men, took part in various engagements and experienced many dangerous situations. They were forced to endure terrible suffering caused by insufficient food, intense cold, bad boots and 'wretchedly' inadequate clothing. Kirwan was a severe disciplinarian and expected the same of his officers and men, which contributed to the survival of many of them on the field of battle. He was fortunate with his officers: one of them, F. McAlevey, had served in the French Foreign Legion for many years and was welcomed by the men. Several of the non-commissioned officers, and indeed the troops themselves, had already seen service in the British army. Sergeant Anthony Donnellan, also from Galway, was the most respected non-commissioned officer among the troops. His conduct in action brought him to the notice of Kirwan and he was recommended for a commission for his gallantry, but because his command of the French language was limited, he was refused. Some time later Donnellan was wounded in the Battle of Montbéliard and was reported missing during the subsequent retreat. He was never seen or heard of again.

Kirwan's Irish company then travelled to Bruges under orders to join forces with the Fifth Battalion of the French *Légion Étrangère* (Foreign Legion). This regiment had suffered severely in the first Battle of Orleans, where it had lost over 1,000 men in the first days of fighting. The

Irish company received a warm welcome from the French officers. Over the following weeks the weather conditions were brutal, the men's boots and bedding were inadequate and the meagre rations added to the misery of the troops. On Christmas Eve the temperature dropped to seventeen degrees below zero and the blankets issued to the troops were not large enough to cover them. While this created problems, it was the boots that caused most of the suffering. Sand and small stones found their way over the miserably low uppers and chafed against the men's skin, causing sores. The frost then literally gnawed holes into the men's feet as deep and as wide as a 'five shilling piece'. In some instances, the men cut away the portion of the boots that was causing the problems, but being exposed to the severe cold, the sores grew bigger and became more painful. Others threw away their 'wretched excuses' for boots and marched barefoot and bleeding. A few men cut up their clothing to wrap around their feet. However, most of the soldiers were actually afraid to take off the boots, as their feet would swell, rendering it impossible to put them on again. Their first action following enemy engagements was to remove the boots from the Prussian dead, as they were better equipped. The men were constantly stalked by hunger and this was apparent in their gaunt faces. In extreme cases, soldiers even committed suicide rather than continue to endure such misery. Some of the French soldiers were executed for stealing food.

While Kirwan was a very disciplined and strict commander, he handled situations differently from the French. He realised that the French were executing men for offences that during peace time would only warrant a few weeks in a guardhouse. Rather than execute his men for such offences, Kirwan assigned them extra duties. It is to his credit that offences in the Irish company were extremely rare: the men, although suffering in brutal winter conditions, were well trained and well behaved.

Amidst all the terrible hardships and dangers of the campaign, the Irish seem to have maintained a good sense of humour. An officer is reported to have said, 'Hold up your head, soldier!' to one of the men who had just ducked beneath a makeshift parapet during a sharp engagement.

'I will, Sir, when there's room for it up there,' he replied, half laughing.

It was during the last couple of weeks of the war that the Irish experienced the most severe fighting. On 7 January 1871 their regiment was sent to relieve Belfort and attempt to force the war into Germany. For three days they took part in bitter fighting around Montbéliard, taking many casualties. Kirwan was wounded but continued to command his men and having received medical treatment he quickly recovered. When the French army was forced to retreat, it was Kirwan's company and the Fifth Battalion who took up the rearguard. His orders from the French commanding officer were simple:

> You will follow us into the open; it is there we shall possibly encounter the Germans, for they are massed on three sides of us. If we are attacked in force, we shall have to fight; but if only slightly, you will engage the enemy and give us time to get away.[185]

---

185 'An Irish Company in the War of 1870–71', *The Tuam Herald*, 16 October 1915.

Thus, the Irish were last to leave the battlefield, which was looked upon as a considerable honour by both the French and indeed the Prussians. That night they covered the French retreat. They were moving through a wooded area and 'Silence, silence!' was the whispered order from the officers, as the Prussians were nearby. The effort to march quietly was awkward, but the least noise would betray their position to the enemy. There was a sense of relief as they were about to emerge from the woods, but suddenly, like a clap of thunder, volley after volley of gunfire passed through their ranks. They pulled back into the woods, returning fire haphazardly as they moved. The Prussians hesitated in their advance, which gave Kirwan time to regroup, but vigorous fire was sustained by both sides, each aiming at the flash from each other's guns. The bullets from the enemy rifles cut through the trees and hissed all around the woods. The remaining French troops disappeared under cover of darkness and the Irish, now alone, were reduced to about sixty-five rifles. The firing stopped after a time with neither side gaining any ground. The Irish remained in their positions until shortly before daybreak and then moved quietly away, leaving a 'ghastly field' behind them.

It was a nerve-racking retreat. Every finger held a trigger awaiting the order to fire as they expected to see the dark-blue uniforms of the Prussians bursting out of the gloom. The Irish soon caught up with the retreating French battalion. Then, foodless and in many cases shoeless, this small band of men continued their disastrous retreat. The main French army, ahead of them, had depleted the countryside of supplies. Horseflesh was the only food the men had had to eat for days. The woods and fields were strewn with corpses and the debris of war; broken wagons and damaged guns were everywhere.

With empty haversacks and heavy hearts, the Irish company continued its harassed retreat. Fortunately, Kirwan had trained his men well. There was no disorder, no broken ranks, no crowding: everything was conducted with soldierly and professional precision. Skirmishers moved close on both flanks, occasionally turning to check if the enemy were advancing. Discipline was as rigidly enforced as always, but famine had done its work on this group of emaciated and ragged troops. During the retreat their numbers were further depleted, and by the end of January 1871 they could only muster some fifty rifles. By 2 February the surviving French and Irish joined up with the remaining French army and prepared to defend themselves, as an attack was imminent.

The Prussian cavalry soon made its appearance, formed a line and charged. Fusillade after fusillade opened up on the advancing horsemen and many saddles were emptied that day. Nevertheless, the advance continued as additional cavalry were deployed in the attack. The following is a description of the charge by one of the Irish defenders:

> Many a brave fellow for the last time spurred his charger onwards as from the sheltered slopes of bush and break, the riflemen sent volley after volley into the advancing squadrons. Horses and riders rolled upon the earth and rider-less steeds rushed frantically over the plain sniffing the air with wide distended nostrils.[186]

---

186 *Ibid.*

While the Irish and their French comrades defended well, elsewhere the Prussians were taking French positions, eventually forcing a total surrender. One of the senior French commanders, Marshal Bazaine, had already surrendered at Metz on 27 October 1870, which had effectively taken 173,000 men out of the war. Paris was under siege and its citizens attempted to fight off the enemy with crude and makeshift weapons. There was widespread starvation and the people were reduced to eating cats, dogs and even rats.[187]

On 18 January 1871 William I, the Prussian king, was crowned Emperor of Germany in the Hall of Mirrors at Versailles. Paris surrendered the following day. However, the Irish troops were not aware of the widespread surrender and, along with the remaining French Fifth Battalion, they faced the Prussians across the battlefield. The bayonets of both sides glittered in the morning sunshine when suddenly a French cavalry officer, bearing a white flag, rode furiously towards the combat lines. He carried with him an urgent dispatch announcing the surrender. The troops had been fighting three days longer than anywhere else in France and it seems that it was the Irish who fired the last shots of the war.

Following the surrender, the Irish troops, having won the admiration of the French, were offered positions in the new French army that was being assembled, but they declined. They were then issued with a month's salary and sailing tickets for Ireland. They all accepted, with the exception of one unnamed officer, who decided to remain in France. On

---

187 Glover, *Warfare*, p. 149.

30 March 1871 the troops set sail for Ireland via Liverpool. The Treaty of Frankfurt, signed on 10 May 1871, officially ended the Franco-Prussian War. The Prussians were now the undisputed supreme military power in Europe.

Captain Kirwan stayed on in England for some years after the war before returning to Galway. He became a devoted supporter of Home Rule and a close friend of Isaac Butt and Charles Stewart Parnell, helping to organise Home Rule rallies and meetings throughout Ireland and England. In 1876 he went to Canada and later travelled to New York, where he died in 1899. He married and had one daughter, but very little is known about his family. However, an ancestor of his was known as 'Dick of the Sword' and also fought for France in the ranks of the Irish Brigade at the Battle of Fontenoy in 1745.[188]

Oranmore: A Smugglers' Haven

During the eighteenth century, restrictions on Irish trade led to Oranmore, a small village on the outskirts of Galway, becoming the main market town for smugglers. There was an export duty of 4s per pound on manufactured cloth and 5d on wool. The smugglers were running goods out through Galway Bay by night to France, where they

---

188 'Irish Company in the War'.

were sold for higher prices. They always returned with ships loaded with silk, brandy, lace and a variety of other items. Some ships also sailed to America to ply their trade.

The most famous smugglers of this period included Captains Lynch and Yorke, both Galwaymen, and Captains Delamaine and Farrell, both French. Their ships had a reputation for speed and it was said that no government vessel could outrun them. The smugglers were often toasted at balls in places as far away as Birr. The following toast testifies to the success of the Oranmore smuggling trade: 'Here's to Captain Lynch, shod, hosed, gartered, flounced, dressed, lace-cloaked, and hooded, the fairest, and prettiest, and the best ladies in Europe, all here tonight, a testimony to his good taste.'

People came from all over the country, many from as far away as Ulster, to trade in Oranmore and avoid the high government taxes. At the time it was known by a number of names, including 'Burke Town', 'The Charters Town' and 'The Town of Lodging Houses'. The latter name would indicate that there was a high number of visitors. By the middle of the eighteenth century Oranmore was thriving, and it boasted of two tanyards and a cooperage, which was owned by a man named Vesey, who had made a fortune from the salted meat and hide trade. There was also a boat builder's yard, a timber works, a bone button factory, two rope works, a scotch mill, a woollen mill, block and bobbin yard, and various other industries. These businesses provided work for many 'expelled Galway citizens', most of whom were Catholics suffering under the Penal Laws. It was 1804 before Catholics were freely admitted to Galway city. The success of the Oranmore flax and woollen industry also gave employment to thirty-one

Presbyterian families and almost twice as many Protestant families.

During the nineteenth century an old Claddagh man gave a description of Oranmore at the time of the smugglers, which was passed down to him by his father:

> In those days you could see on a Sunday in Oran hundreds of big, brown-bearded young men, dressed up in grand, thick, blue broadcloth trousers and blue double-breasted coats with white cambric mufflers on every man as white as dribbling snow … they were mostly blue water seamen.[189]

The emblem of the smugglers was a crooked knife, which was supposed to give safe passage to anyone under its protection. This tradition originated in County Kerry, when the O'Connell family issued an English army officer with such a knife, which was actually a garden pruning knife and was very rare at the time. It seems that this type of knife was associated with the family and because it was unusual it was easy to recognise. This token gave the officer genuine protection through the 'wild districts' of Kerry and later became a smugglers' symbol.

The American War of Independence in 1776 threatened the smuggling trade as security on various American ports was stepped up. By this time other smugglers had joined the ranks in Oranmore. They included Captains Comerford, Purcell, Dominic and McCarthy. Even the contraband agent for Oranmore, a man named Kelly, owned a half-share in a ship running goods to and from the West Indies. The

---

189 'Oranmore', *The Connacht Tribune*, 15 October 1921.

smugglers became even more daring and the illegal trading continued. However, it was the French Revolution that signalled an end to the great smuggling era in Oranmore, and for this the smugglers were partly to blame.

On 11 July 1792, a vessel, the *Minerva*, arrived in Galway, having sailed from England with news of the dreadful situation in revolutionary France. On the night of 16 July, three ships arrived off Roscam, having sailed from the West Indies. They were the *Mary Jewel* under Captain Lynch, the *Erandre* under Captain Dominic and the *Irish Sea* under Captain Yorke. Some 200 men arrived from Oranmore and quickly unloaded the cargo. The three captains were approached by Dr Dillon, a former president of the Irish College and coadjutor bishop of Kilmacduagh, who pleaded with the smugglers to sail to France and rescue certain religious figures and members of the old French aristocratic families from the guillotine. (Dillon was an aristocrat, being a member of the Clonbrock family. He was living in Kilcornan near Oranmore and was familiar with the smugglers.) The smugglers agreed to support Dillon and the following morning they set sail for France. They successfully rescued a number of people, but as they sailed for home three French ships – a cornette, a brig and a sloop – confronted them. In the ensuing battle, the smugglers sank the brig and severely damaged the cornette. They boarded the sloop and took anything of value off the ship before sailing for home.

Two days later the French sank *The Patriot Arm*, under Captain Purcell, thus sending out a very clear message to the smugglers that they were now enemies of the French revolutionaries and would be treated as such. The British government offered Captains Lynch, Yorke and Dominic 'privateers' licences', which would allow them to trade legitimately, but they refused and continued to smuggle refugees out of France.

By now it was believed that a French invasion of Ireland would take place. One of the smugglers' great supporters among the aristocracy was Erroll Blake (Lord Wallscourt) of Ardfry House near Oranmore. Over the years they had enriched Blake through their illegal activities and in turn he had proved a good friend. Blake was a United Irishman and under the threat of French invasion tried to enlist the support of the smugglers. However, the smugglers would not be cajoled into backing the French at this stage and would not support the United Irishmen either because of their strong connection with the French. Thus Erroll Blake, their great friend, now became their great foe. The smugglers also refused to support England against France. Many fierce encounters followed between the smugglers and the French, resulting in the loss of men and ships on both sides. It is believed that when a French expedition led by General Humbert arrived in 1798 in support of the Irish rebellion they avoided Galway Bay because of the smugglers. They instead decided to sail into Killala Bay in County Mayo.

The smugglers were in a sense the architects of their own demise. Such conflicts meant that trade markets and routes were closed to them almost immediately, leaving Oranmore devastated and deserted within a short time. A decision was taken by the leading captains to emigrate to the Americas, but before leaving many visited the last resting place of their ancestors. An eyewitness later wrote a description of the sailors before departure. One of them he mentioned by name as Philip Kelly, the second mate on the *Mary Jewel*, and described how he visited his family grave in the old cemetery in Oranmore and took from his pocket a small velvet purse embroidered with a silver cross. He then proceeded to fill the purse with earth from the grave. All of those visiting the cemetery did the same, and all the time the women wept. The reason for this ritual was that regardless of where the emigrants died, in a foreign land or at sea, the purses of earth would be buried with them, thus uniting them with their home and ancestors. The smugglers then sailed for the West Indies, taking their women and children with them, and consequently ending the very lucrative smuggling trade around Galway Bay.[190]

Plague, Leprosy and Disease

In 1541 a hospital dedicated to St Bridget was founded for the poor of the town at Prospect Hill. It was located close to the narrow lane leading from Prospect Hill to the present-day St Patrick's Church. The hospital was funded by the burgesses of the town who in turn would send a maid or servant out to collect alms for the upkeep of the hospital every Sabbath. Two years after the hospital was founded

---

190 *Ibid.*

hundreds of people died of a sweating disease or sickness that raged in the town. The origin of this highly contagious and lethal disease is unknown.

St Bridget's subsequently served as a leper hospital, as lepers were strictly forbidden to enter the walled city. Only their superior or custodian, who did not suffer from the disease, was permitted to enter the town. He attracted the attention of the inhabitants by ringing a bell and then collected alms to support those suffering in the hospital. This position was normally filled by compulsion or by generous inducements to anyone willing to take the risk of working as custodian of the lepers.[191] There is a so-called leper's gallery located inside St Nicholas' Collegiate Church in the centre of the town, which according to tradition was the place where sufferers of this infamous disease attended religious services. However, this is merely a legend as lepers were never permitted to enter the city.[192]

The bubonic plague struck Galway for the first time in 1629. The plague was introduced to the town by ships returning from Spain carrying unwelcome rats and their parasitic fleas, which spread the disease quickly in some of the overcrowded areas of the city. The plague was transmitted to humans chiefly by fleas from the infected rats.

The plague had been brought to Europe in the fourteenth century. In 1327 the Mongol army failed to take the Genoese trading post of Kaffa in the Crimea after laying siege to it. To make matters worse, the Mongols were decimated

---

191 Henry, *Role of Honour*, pp. 60–1.
192 O'Dowd, *Old and New Galway*, p. 78.

by a mysterious disease. Before leaving, they mounted the still-warm bodies of their dead on to giant catapults and hurled them over the walls of the town, causing the plague to spread. The Genoese defenders boarded their ships to escape from the plague-ridden town, but many of them had already caught the deadly disease and carried it with them. This had horrendous consequences when the ships reached European ports, and the plague spread through the various towns and cities.[193]

The bubonic plague is often referred to as the Black Death because it caused spots of blood under the skin to turn black; but the naming also reflected its devastating effect on society. Symptoms usually developed quickly and the victim would not generally live very long, suffering from chills, fever, headache, body pains and swelling of the lymph glands. Between 1603 and 1665 more than 150,000 people died from this disease in London. According to some sources, the children's nursery rhyme 'Ring a Ring o' Roses' owes it origin to the victims of the bubonic plague.[194] It seems that one symptom was a circular, rosy discolouring of the skin. A 'pocket full of posies' and the following words possibly referred to a herbal remedy, a fit of sneezing and falling down – death.

---

193 'The Black Death: Scourge of Medieval Europe', *Awake*, 8 February 2000, p. 22.

194 Henry, *Role of Honour*, p. 66.

Fire at Menlo Castle

Menlo Castle, located on the banks of the River Corrib, was the ancestral home of the Blake family, who had lived there from *c.* 1600. The castle was strategically positioned and was occupied for a short time by the Cromwellians during the mid-seventeenth century, but was later returned to the Blakes. Over the centuries the family developed a good relationship with their tenants and the villagers of Menlo. They were also respected by the people of the town, in particular the sporting fraternity, as they opened their grounds to the public every year for 'Maying in Menlo', an extremely popular event. During this festival the estate became the venue for all kinds of sports – athletics, yachting, tennis and rowing. Music and dancing also featured. Boats set out from the town carrying passengers and participants alike, all looking forward to their time at Menlo Castle. However, this all ended in the early hours of 26 July 1910, when a disastrous fire broke out.[195]

The owners of the castle, Sir Valentine and Lady Blake, were away in Dublin at the time. Sir Valentine was having minor surgery carried out on his eyes. Their eldest daughter, Ellen Blake, an invalid, was the only member of the family in the castle that night.[196] Also present when the fire broke

---

195 'The Fire at Menlo Castle', *Galway Advertiser*, 9 July 2009.
196 'When Fire Destroyed Menlo Castle', *Galway Advertiser*, 9 March 2000.

out were two servant girls, Anne Browne and Delia Earley, and the groom, James Kirwan. Ellen Blake, who suffered from mood swings, was in the habit of having an oil lamp in her room. Before leaving for Dublin, Lady Blake had told the servant girls to remove the lamp from Ellen's room before they retired to bed. However, when they tried to take the oil lamp away as instructed, Ellen ordered them to leave the room and go to bed immediately. A short time later she called them back and said that she would entertain them by playing the piano. She played a number of tunes and then suddenly stopped and ordered the girls to bed again. Their room was in the attic at the top of the castle. As they prepared for bed they again became worried about the oil lamp and made their way back down the stairs very quietly, but Ellen Blake was still awake, hugging her pet, a black cat. Being unable to remove the lamp, they returned to their room.

Anne Browne awoke at about 4.00 a.m. Her throat was dry and hot and she smelled smoke. She jumped out of bed and tried to call her friend, who at first did not want to move. There was a sudden crash outside the room and when the girls opened the bedroom door they could see smoke and flames bellowing up through the castle. The terrified girls could see that there was no escape by the stairs as the flames had already taken hold. They began shouting and screaming for help and ran back into the room, making their way out through a dormer window and on to the roof.[197]

---

197 'The Girl who was Carried on a Door', *Galway Advertiser*, 8 March 2007.

At about 5.40 a.m., James Kirwan, who was sleeping on the first floor and just above the main door of the castle, was awakened by the sound of voices. He knew that it was Anne and Delia, but for some reason he thought they were playing a joke. He remained in bed until a few minutes after 6.00 a.m., when he began to smell smoke. He leaped out of bed and ran to the door. Upon opening it a sudden rush of smoke and flames blinded him. There was no way of reaching the ground floor as the staircase was ablaze and it was then that he realised that the two girls were screaming because they were trapped on the roof. He slammed his door shut, grabbed his clothes, smashed the window and began climbing down the ivy attached to the castle walls. It broke away and he fell to the ground, but was not injured. He could see that the whole castle was in flames and ran quickly to the yard at the side. It was then that he saw the two girls on the roof, still screaming. He called out that he was going for help and ran to the gate lodge where he alerted the gardener, James Ward. While Ward was getting dressed, Kirwan ran and found another man, Michael Faherty, from the village and the three men returned together. They secured a ladder, but it was too short; they tried throwing a rope up to the girls, but they could not catch it. Then they began spreading hay, hoping that it would save the girls if they had to jump.[198]

By this time the girls' clothes were beginning to burn as the flames broke through the roof. Although it was some forty feet to the ground, the girls had no choice but to jump

---

198 'Appalling Fire at Menlo Castle', *The Connacht Tribune*, 30 July 1910.

in the hope of landing safely on the hay. Delia Earley went first and was killed instantly as she landed on her head.[199] Anne Browne jumped almost immediately afterwards and landed on the hay, on her hands and feet. When Kirwan ran to her aid, she said, 'Oh Kirwan! I am killed' and fainted. Kirwan then saddled a horse and rode first into the town for help, and from there he went to Castlegar for a priest.[200]

Once the alarm was raised firemen from Renmore military barracks under Major Sarsfield made their way to Menlo. At the same time the town brigade was rushing to the scene. However, by the time both units arrived, the entire castle was engulfed in flames. By this stage there was no hope of saving Ellen Blake, as she was trapped inside the inferno. It was later reported that one of the men saw something black moving through the flames – it was believed to be the cat. Anne Browne regained her senses as the priest was anointing her. There was a loud crashing sound as the interior of the castle collapsed. Anne was lying too close to the castle wall to be safe, but when people tried to move her she cried out in absolute agony from her injuries and severe burns. Eventually the people located a door and lifted the unfortunate girl onto the makeshift stretcher, which was then placed on the back of a horse-drawn cart. The journey to the infirmary in Prospect Hill was agonising and took hours, the cart's driver having to stop often as Anne was in so much pain. From time to time she was given cold buttermilk to drink by farmers on their

199 'The Fire at Menlo Castle'.
200 'Appalling Fire at Menlo Castle'.

way to the market in Galway that morning.[201]

It was not known for sure how the fire started, but it was believed to have been caused by the oil lamp in Ellen Blake's room. No trace of her body was ever found. Delia Earley was from Galway and was just twenty-five years of age when she lost her life. Anne Browne spent five months in hospital and was released into the care of her friends, the Cloonan family in Bohermore. She later emigrated to the United States, where she remained for the rest of her life. However, almost seventy years later, Anne contacted local historian the late Maurice Semple after reading one of his books and gave him the details of what had happened that terrible night.[202] On 6 August 1910 it was announced that the castle was to be rebuilt, but this did not happen as the Blake family had already moved away.[203] Over the years, the condition of the ruin deteriorated. Then, in 2000, a very generous offer of £3.75 million was made by a businessman, Noel Smith, to Galway City Council to rebuild the castle. However, because of the obstacles in the path of the restoration work, the redevelopment did not happen.[204] The ruined castle is now destined to fall into a heap of rubble and with it will go an extremely important part of Galway's history.

---

201 'Girl who was Carried on a Door'.
202 Semple, *Reflections on Lough Corrib*, p. 107
203 'The Castle to be Rebuilt', *The Connacht Tribune*, 6 August 1910.
204 'Objectors in Ruins over Menlo Restoration Project', *Galway Advertiser*, 27 July 2000.

The Isolation Hospital

In 1895 the Port Sanitary Authority had a temporary isolation hospital constructed at Renmore Point. It was located on land leased from the governors of the Erasmus Smith Schools and Major Wilson Lynch of Renmore House. By 1906 the authorities had decided to negotiate a deal to have a permanent hospital on the site. Following a number of meetings, they secured a forty-year lease at £1 per annum. Two years later the Port Sanitary Intercepting Hospital, more commonly known as the 'Isolation Hospital', opened. It was designed as a sailors' quarantine hospital for the treatment of such diseases as cholera, smallpox, scurvy and beri-beri, and it had twenty beds. However, throughout its existence it only had to provide accommodation for three patients: sailors from south-west Africa who arrived in Galway in February 1911. It was suspected they were suffering from beri-beri, and after they had recovered sufficiently, they were discharged. Two of the sailors boarded a ship, leaving Galway, but the third decided to remain, becoming an embarrassment to the town because of his drinking escapades. He was known as the 'beri-beri man'. The town guardians had to pay two nurses and a cook to look after him during his stay as he was still living in the hospital. One member of the local authority claimed that the man had been suffering from the effects of excessive drinking and not beri-beri. Eventually he was placed on board a ship leaving Galway harbour.

Sometime later a family moved into the hospital and lived there for a number of years. They vacated the building in the early 1960s and it fell into disuse. In 1966 it burned down and remained derelict for a number of years. The cause of the fire is unknown. Eventually the Isolation Hospital was demolished and the once-familiar building disappeared from the Galway landscape.[205]

The Old County Infirmary

T ucked neatly away inside the foyer of the County Hall in Prospect Hill are part of the remains of the old County Infirmary. Hundreds of people pass through this building every day, most of them unaware that the internal stone wall is actually the façade of the old infirmary. The County Infirmary opened in June 1802, replacing an older hospital in Abbeygate Street. Conditions were so appalling in the old infirmary that they even shocked John Howard, a noted philanthropist who had witnessed the horrifying conditions in the prisons and lazarettos of Europe.[206]

The new infirmary at Prospect Hill was three storeys high and over 40 metres in length. There was an imposing

---

205 Murray, *Galway: a Medico-Social History*, pp. 138–9.
206 S. McGuire, 'The County Infirmary', *Galway Reader*, vol. 3, nos 1, 2, 1950, pp. 74, 76.

cut-stone doorway giving access to a spacious hallway running the full length of the building. The ground floor consisted of a boardroom, housekeeper's room and nurse's bedroom on the left of the entrance and on the right there was a waiting room, surgery, kitchen and scullery. A stone staircase gave access to the first- and second-floor patient wards. There was also a 'dead house', where the remains of those who died in the hospital were held until their families removed them for burial. A large paved yard at the rear of the building contained a coach house and stables, and a 'cesspool' was located a mere eighteen feet from the main water supply.[207] There was also a children's burial ground at the rear of the building. Dr James Veitch, a Scotsman, was the first superintendent of the infirmary. He was also the first Catholic to be appointed to such a position in Ireland. Robert Ffrench of Monivea Castle was appointed to look after the finances. The following fourteen rules or regulations of the infirmary were strictly enforced:

I: No person can be admitted as (intern) patient of the hospital who does not produce a letter of recommendation from a governor or governess of the infirmary.

II: The hours of general attendance at the hospital are from 11 to 12 o'clock every day. All out-patients to attend at those hours. No out-patient to proceed further than the hall of the hospital without orders from the surgeon.

III: The days of admission (only) on Mondays and Thursdays, except in cases of accident.

IV: The patient, upon his or her appearance in the hall of the hospital, at the hours and days above-mentioned, and

---

207   Murray, *Galway: a Medico-Social History*, p. 60.

producing the recommendation, will be immediately inserted upon the books of the hospital.

V: Each patient, after being inserted on the books, to be taken to the bathroom to be well washed and cleaned by the person appointed for that purpose, and the barber directed to attend; afterwards to be taken to the vesting room and dressed in the hospital clothing, and directed to the ward and bed appointed by the surgeon; and on his or her dismissal their own clothing be given to him, and the hospital clothing delivered up to the proper person appointed, to be well washed and fumigated, and put upon the proper number in the vesting room.

VI: The nurses to count over the bed clothes and clothing, etc., to the patient; and are to be responsible that he or she leaves everything in the same state, allowing for the necessary tear and wear; and no patient (except allowed by the surgeon) to visit the other wards; if found in any but their own, to be immediately dismissed from the hospital.

VII: No patient to be allowed to spit or dirty the walls or floors of the house, as spitting boxes and bed pots are provided for the purpose; and no smoking of pipes allowed on any account in the wards.

VIII: Immediately upon the bell ringing, every patient that is able (or who is ordered by the surgeon) are to attend in the dressing room.

IX: Any patient who acts impertinent to the housekeeper or nurses to be immediately dismissed, and to be reported to the governor or governess who recommended him or her.

X: All medicine to be given by the surgeon or nurses; and they are immediately to report should they refuse either medicine or diet as directed.

XI: The wards of the hospital to be washed and fumigated twice a week, and oftener if necessary.

XII: The housekeeper to visit the wards twice a day and to report any deviation from the above rules, as she is responsible for the cleanliness of the whole hospital; and no filth or excrement of any kind to remain one minute in the patients' ward.

XIII: The nurses or housekeeper are to see the patients take their meals, according to the dietary annexe; and the patients to report any neglect or deficiency in their diet first to the nurses, then to the housekeeper, and if immediate redress is not granted, to the surgeon.

XIV: The rules and regulations to be read to each patient on admission to the house; and their name, age, and disease, posted up on the head of their bed.

The meals consisted of the following for those on a 'Full Diet'.

Breakfast: One quart of good stirabout, with one pint of new milk, or one quart of sour ditto; – the same that night.

Dinner: One pound of good household loaf bread, and one quart of new milk, four days in the week; – and a half pound of boiled meat, one quarter stone of potatoes, with as much broth and vegetables as they can eat, the other three days.[208]

Many victims of the outbreak of Asiatic cholera that reached Galway in May 1832 died in the infirmary. Within a month, the disease had killed 275 people.

In 1892 the building was officially named the Galway Hospital, but it continued to be known locally as 'the infirmary'.[209] In January 1900 a serious flu epidemic swept through Galway. Such was the scale of the outbreak that funerals became an everyday occurrence throughout the city.[210] In the same year the Convent of Mercy nuns took charge of the nursing care at the infirmary, but by 1924 it had

---

208 McGuire, 'County Infirmary', pp. 74–6.

209 Murray, *Galway: a Medico-Social History*, pp. 53, 67.

210 'The Influenza', *The Galway Express*, 6 January 1900.

been phased out.[211] From 1926–34 it was used as a library by Galway County Council. It then became the county buildings, where much of the everyday business concerning the county was carried out. The old infirmary building was demolished in 1996 to make way for the new County Hall, which opened in 1999. The children's burial ground can still be found in the north-east corner of the car park.

Galway Whiskey

While Galway has always been noted for its wine trade, little is known about its whiskey production. The best-known whiskey in Galway during the nineteenth century was Persse's Galway Whiskey, which was produced at the Nun's Island distillery. Patrick Joyce originally established this distillery to produce Joyce's Whiskey in 1815. The building was five storeys high and situated on a small island formed by the fork in the River Corrib.[212] It seems that sometime later this distillery was bought by another Galway businessman, John Lynch,[213] and closed sometime during the 1830s. In 1840 Burton Persse of Newcastle, a member of the ascendancy family who had properties throughout County

211 Murray, *Galway: a Medico-Social History*, p. 67.
212 'Persse's Galway Whiskey', *Galway Advertiser*, 9 November 1995.
213 'Nun's Island Whiskey', *Galway Advertiser*, 6 August 2009.

Galway, purchased it. These houses included Roxborough, which was the birthplace of Isabella Augusta Persse, who later became Lady Gregory of Coole.[214] Burton Persse lived in Newcastle House during the early nineteenth century as it was close to one of his distilleries. Both the house and distillery were later acquired by University College Galway and no longer exist; the name Distillery Road is the only real indication of their existence.

As Persse already owned two distilleries, the one at Newcastle and another at Newtownsmith, he had the Nun's Island distillery converted into a woollen mill. During the mid 1840s his lease on the Newcastle distillery lapsed and at about that time the woollen industry went into decline. Persse had the Nun's Island mill converted back into a distillery. Shortly afterwards he closed down his Newtownsmith distillery and concentrated his efforts on Nun's Island.[215]

The Nun's Island distillery was certainly built in the ideal place, as according to one contemporary source the enormous surge of water discharged from the river was strong enough to power all the mills in Manchester. Water hoses were placed throughout the building in case of fire. Around the large triangular courtyard there was a series of buildings including a brew house connected to the still house, which had three stills capable of holding 10,000 gallons of spirits. There were also five warehouses in the complex. Two of the buildings had five floors and were devoted to the storage of

214 'Persse's Galway Whiskey'.
215 'Nun's Island Whiskey'.

corn for malting purposes. There was a kiln attached to these buildings and the malt depot was situated at the rear of the general offices. The malt and dried corn was pulverised in the stone loft by means of a water wheel. Once the whiskey was produced, it was stored close by until it was ready for delivery. The spirit store contained a 12,000-gallon storage vat. As horse and cart was the only mode of transport, there were also stables for the horses and a cart shed, and the tradesmen on the site included a smithy, a joiner and painters. The distillery proved very successful and by the late 1880s the annual production of Galway Whiskey was about 400,000 gallons.[216] The distillery employed over 100 people directly and many more found employment with the various suppliers.[217]

During the 1840s another whiskey distillery, Burke's, opened approximately where Jury's Hotel stands today and was commonly known as the Quarter Barrel Distillery. However, it only survived until the 1860s and posed no real threat to Persse's Galway Whiskey.[218] Persse's was noted for its quality and was advertised as 'The leading Whiskey of the day.' A leaflet promoting its virtues condemned other whiskey producers for using sugar, molasses, beetroot and potatoes, which they said produced a flavourless product. The writer also accused the distillers of producing a low-cost spirit and then mixing it with the good-quality Galway Whiskey, and flavouring it with various chemical essences.

216 'Persse's Galway Whiskey'.
217 'Nun's Island Whiskey'.
218 'Synge the Snapper', *Galway Advertiser*, 14 July 2005.

The result was a crude, harsh, poisonous liquor. The leaflet acclaimed the qualities of Persse's whiskey, stating that it was produced from home-grown Irish barley using water unrivalled for its softness and purity and under the constant and close observation of experts in the art of distilling. 'No wonder,' it stated, 'Galway whiskey has come to be looked on as an ideal beverage, as a safe stimulant and a most valued medicine.'[219] The quality of Persse's Galway Whiskey is borne out by the fact that in 1882 the price of a glass of whiskey was 3½ pence, but a glass of Persse's finest could be sold for 5 pence.[220]

Under the heading 'Another Triumph for Galway Whiskey', it was announced in 1898 that Persse's of Galway had, after an open competition, secured the contract to supply all the Irish whiskey to Crystal Palace for three years. The contract also included the bars of the Barnum and Bailey circus show. The report continued, 'It is almost needless to remark that the whiskey to be supplied at those popular places of entertainment will be of the same age and quality as supplied to the gentlemen of the House of Commons.'[221]

By the end of the nineteenth century visitors to Galway were favourably impressed by the improvements to the town and its business establishments. In October 1900 *The Galway Express* stated that 'the principle industry of which the citizens are justly proud is in the manufacture of

---

219 'The Old Galway', *Galway Advertiser*, 14 December 1995.

220 Naughton, *History of St Francis Parish*, p. 40.

221 'Another Triumph for Galway Whiskey', *The Galway Vindicator*, 14 December 1898.

Persse's famous whiskey'. However, there was a tendency by Galway publicans to try to sell off their own cheaper brands of whiskey as Persse's brew. In December 1902 the distillery issued a warning of the legal consequences that would follow if people were caught involved in such activity, and it is believed that this was a contributing factor in the closure of Persse's Distillery in 1908.

Persse's Distillery memorabilia has become very collectable and valuable. The bar mirrors with the distinctive image of the distillery in the centre are rare, as are the labelled whiskey bottles. In 2002 a dealer placed a bottle of Persse's Galway Whiskey for sale and advertised it as 'the rarest bottle of whiskey in the world'. It could be purchased for £100,000. It seems that it eventually sold for a sum close to the asking price. There is some Persse memorabilia housed in Galway City Museum.[222]

The Galway Watchmen

The Galway Watchmen were formed in the mid-nineteenth century to prevent street crime – a similar role to the volunteer police reserves today.

By the 1820s Galway's stocks and pillories were in a state of neglect and had fallen out of use. The loss of these

---

222 'Nun's Island Whiskey'.

deterrents to petty crime, vandalism and violent behaviour brought its own problems.[223] In 1826 *The Galway Weekly Advertiser* reported that violent crime continued to increase, with people being brutally beaten on the streets almost every night. It was reported that some of the attacks were such that they would make 'humanity shudder'. The reporter complained that even the pickpockets who were arrested and interrogated were being let loose on the streets within hours for want of a magistrate to take any real action against them and commit them to prison. The report warned that many valuable lives may be lost if something was not done to prevent these criminals from terrorising people in the town. The aphorism 'some things never change' springs to mind.[224]

There seems to have been a somewhat ad hoc approach to many areas of policing and subsequent judgements. In April 1854 eighteen youngsters ranging in ages from ten to fifteen were brought before Judge J. B. Kernan on charges of playing football in the streets. 'The offence was fully proved, and the juvenile delinquents (or guttersnipes as they were often referred to) were sentenced to pay a fine of 2s 6d each or go to jail for a week' (an alternative doubtless embraced as money was scarce).[225] Yet serious crime was not being tackled and there was a call from the public to keep the streets clear of those 'who offend the eye and ear'.

There were appalling scenes of 'drunken abominations –

---

223   S. McGuire, 'Law and Order in Galway', *Galway Reader*, vol. 4, nos 2, 3, 1954, p. 65.

224   'State of Galway', *The Galway Weekly Advertiser and Connaught Journal*, 9 December 1826.

225   'The Ballplaying Nuisance', *The Galway Vindicator*, 29 April 1854.

the cursing and blasphemy of those unfortunate creatures who are lost to all sense of shame'. Even during the day, people suffered by being jostled and abused on the footpaths as they made their way to and from work or shopping.[226] The situation was such that by the 1840s there was a serious need for extra policing.

This led to the town commissioners introducing a new force, the Galway Watchmen, to assist the police and prevent crime and trouble in the streets. This seemed like an excellent idea, especially as most of the volunteers were aware of the identity of the troublemakers. They did have some initial success; however, this was with boys playing football and petty thieves. Things were very different when it came to violent gangs or individuals fighting. It seems that the very purpose of the force's formation was more or less ignored by the Watchmen. This can be seen from an account of disturbances in the heart of the town that occurred on 14 June 1861 when the population of Abbeygate Street was disturbed by a violent group causing mayhem. Their weapons of choice included pokers, tongs, knives and sticks, resulting in a number of men having to be carried away 'bleeding and senseless'. Following the street battle, the residents complained that members of the Galway Watchmen had been present but would not get involved in the fight or indeed even try to prevent the bloodshed. When one of them was asked why he didn't try to stop the fighting, he replied that only a fool would have gotten involved.

A report was published following the fight stating

---

226 'Street Nuisances', *The Galway Vindicator*, 24 August 1861.

that the Galway Watchmen were 'perfectly useless' in the prevention of crime and the protection of property. When they witnessed a row, it said, they were in the 'habit of disappearing' down alleyways or through nearby doorways. The Watchmen's contribution to crime prevention was minimal and their existence was short lived. It is little wonder that they were forgotten so fast and consigned to the realms of hidden history in the very town they volunteered to protect.[227]

A Public Hanging

John Hurley was convicted of the murder of Catherine Kendrigan. He had struck his victim on the head with a stone and cut her throat. After receiving the death sentence, the prisoner was taken back to his cell in the old Galway jail to await his fate. Because he showed sincere remorse for his crime, the execution was delayed for a short time in the 'faint expectation' that a reprieve might be passed down. Two priests, Frs Commons and Kearney, attended the condemned man and later reported that he 'appeared stricken with repentance' and was engaged in prayer up to his final moments. He even refused to see his sister because he did not wish to be distracted. Shortly before 5 p.m. on 27 August 1853, the

---

227 'What Good are the Watchmen?', *The Galway Vindicator*, 15 June 1861.

prisoner, accompanied by the sub-sheriff, prison officers and flanked by the two priests, walked with a firm step from the condemned cell. In the press room he recited the responses and litanies of the death services with apparently astonishing firmness and fervour, although this must have been a dreadful ordeal for him. He appeared resigned to his fate. The following is an account of the man's last moments:

As he knelt in prayer, he was apparently undisturbed by the hoarse murmur of the surging multitude outside, the executioner approached and pinned his arms, and though the muscles of his face retied their tension, and his features were unmoved, a convulsive tremor passed through his limbs, after which he resumed his devotions, which, weighed with the spiritual exhortations and prayers of the clergymen continued until after six o'clock, when the executioner adjusted the noose about his neck, and after some further prayers, and after shaking hands with Mr Ryan, governor of the jail, and with those present, he ascended the fatal platform with a firm step. He was accompanied by the clergymen to the platform, and as he signified his intention of addressing the multitude at a gesture from one of the rev. gentlemen, the murmur of the mighty crowd was settled, and then the doomed man said with a firm and unfaltering accent – 'I suffer justly; I acknowledge I am guilty of murder; I am thankful to the people of Galway; I am sorry for the words I said in the courthouse, and I ask you all to pray for me, and I hope that the Lord in Heaven will have mercy on my poor soul.' The Rev. Commons repeated the words, but they were pronounced by the prisoner in a distinct voice, and could be heard at a great distance. After the unhappy man had spoken those words, the executioner withdrew the fatal bolt, and he was launched into eternity. His sufferings were not very protracted; a few spasmodic convulsions and the vital spark of life fled for ever. After the body was suspended for twenty minutes, it was cut down and is, we understand, to be buried in the precincts of the prison.

About two thousand people attended the execution; a large proportion of whom were young boys and girls.[228]

The scaffold was erected outside the entrance to the prison and could be removed when not in use. There was an opening above the prison gate through which the condemned person was led onto the scaffold. This practice continued until the Capital Punishment (Amendment) Act, passed in 1868, put an end to public hangings.[229] In many cases family members were allowed to take away the remains of their relatives for burial after execution.

A survey carried out between 1882 and 1883 stated that Galway had a brutal record for executions, with six prisoners being hanged in four days and an additional five put to death a few days later. However, by this period hangings were taking place behind the prison walls. The following is a description of the gallows in Galway jail:

> The monstrous scaffold had been erected at the south side of the prison yard … The scaffold, built of rough deal planks, was ascended by a flight of sixteen steps. At either side was a strong upright which supported a massive cross-beam of wood. From the latter were suspended three ropes with yawning nooses attached.[230]

The new cathedral now occupies the site of Galway jail.

228 'Execution for Murder', *The Galway Vindicator*, 27 August 1853.

229 J. Mitchell, 'The Prisons of Galway: Background to the Inspector General's Reports, 1796–1818', *Journal of the Galway Archaeological & Historical Society*, vol. 49, 1997, p. 18.

230 J. Waldron, *Maamtrasna* (Dublin: Edmund Burke, 1992), p. 150.

William Henry

A Galway Coin Hoard

In 1904 workmen opening an old drain close to Galway Court House discovered eight silver coins dating from the sixteenth and seventeenth centuries. The coins were concealed in a safe place and eventually found their way into the National Museum of Ireland's collection. There was some speculation as to why they were hidden and never retrieved. Because the later coins date from the mid-1640s, it has been suggested that the owner was killed by pestilence, murdered, or sent into forced exile sometime after Cromwellian soldiers took over the city in 1652. While this is a small coin hoard, it is nonetheless very important and interesting as it is the only real hoard of note found in Galway city, and the story of the find is not well known even in Galway. The coins are listed below by monarch and country. The first two coins were specially struck for use in Ireland, making them comparatively rare, and date from May 1536 to October 1537. The Spanish coin appears to have been struck in Mexico between 1555 and 1598. Its inclusion in the hoard is not too surprising, given the area's trading links with Spain. Other hoards from around the county have recorded coins of the same origin.

1. Henry VIII (Ireland): Harp-groat, with crown and initial of Jane Seymour (1536–7).
2. Henry VIII (Ireland): Harp-groat, with crown and initial of Jane Seymour (1536–7).

3. Edward VI (England): Fine Shilling coin (1551–3).
4. Edward VI (England): Fine Shilling coin (1551–3).
5. James I (England): First Coinage Sixpence with thistle design (1603).
6. Charles I (England): Fourth Bust Sixpence with harp design (1632–3).
7. Charles I (England): Third Horseman Half-crown (1645–6).
8. Philip II (Spain): Piece of Eight Reales Dollar (1555–98).[231]

The Knights Templar

In 1312 the Knights Templar were officially disbanded by Pope Clement V and the organisation was suppressed in Galway as elsewhere. It is likely that they played a part in the early commerce of the town.[232] Their convent was located close to the present-day Hotel Meyrick and could have occupied much of the hotel site. The remains of the building are depicted on the 1651 Pictorial Map of Galway.[233] Recent construction work carried out in the Eyre Square area revealed sections of a structure that may have been part of the Templar convent.

231 M. Dolley, 'A Seventeenth-Century Coin-Find from Galway City', *Journal of the Galway Archaeological & Historical Society*, vol. 31, 1964–5, pp. 5–7.
232 W. Henry, *The Shimmering Waste: The Life and Times of Robert O'Hara Burke* (Galway: William Henry, 1997), p. 22.
233 Hardiman, *History of the Town and County*, p. 274.

The Knights Templar were formed in Jerusalem in 1119, officially endorsed around ten years later and played an important role, from a European context, in the Crusades. Thousands were killed during these wars. The Knights were organised similarly to the Cistercians, adopted the Benedictine rule and wore a white robe-like tunic decorated with a red cross. The order became extremely powerful and wealthy, which resulted in the ruling princes of Europe becoming jealous of them. In addition, non-combatant members of the Order played a large role in managing the economic infrastructure of Christendom, innovating early forms of banking, including a cheque for pilgrims to collect cash during journeys.

Many nobles enlisted the support of the Vatican in a bid to discredit the Knights, which eventually led to their demise. Determined to find a way to relieve the Knights of their wealth, King Philip IV of France had Jacques de Molay, the grand master, arrested, falsely accused of heresy and burned at the stake in 1314.[234] In Galway, as in other parts of Europe, the Knights of St John (Hospitaller) of Jerusalem received most of the Templar property and land.

There is a tradition that St Nicholas' Collegiate Church was built on the site of an earlier Knights Templar church. The building of the present church began in 1320 and was believed, at the time, to incorporate part of the earlier ecclesiastical structure. There is also the tradition of the so-called 'crusader's tomb', which some believed was a Templar tomb, located within St Nicholas' church. However, this

234 'Knights Templar', *The World Book Encyclopaedia* (1986).

tomb (of Adam Bures, who is known as 'the Crusader') is of late thirteenth- or early fourteenth-century date.

Following the foundation of the city during the thirteenth century by the de Burgos, many Norman adventurers and merchants had arrived in the fledgling town of Galway. They did not consider themselves Saxon, but rather French – in fact the first language of the city was Norman French.[235] The founding fathers obviously accepted the Knights Templar in Galway, allowing them to build the aforementioned convent near the present-day Eyre Square. There is also a possibility that some members of the de Burgo family were involved in the movement, and the red cross on the de Burgo arms is similar to that emblazoned on the tunic of the Knights.

The de Burgo family has a long history and can trace its descent from Pepin le Vieux, Duke of Anstrasia, who lived in the seventh century AD in what is now France. Charlemagne and Godfrey of Bouillon, one of the leaders of the first military crusade to the Holy Land in AD 1096–9, count amongst his descendants. The de Burgo family coat of arms consists of a yellow shield with a red cross and a lion rampant on the dexter quarter. A chained cat-a-mountain is used as the crest, signifying liberty, vigilance and courage. During the crusade, Godfrey carried a yellow shield into battle. Similarly to all the early coats of arms, his was simple in heraldic terms, with yellow representing the sun, leadership, intelligence and generosity. According to tradition, the red cross was granted to Godfrey by Richard I (the Lionheart) after de Burgo killed a Saracen chief in

235 Hardiman, *History of the Town and County*, p. 274.

battle. Richard dipped his fingers in the blood of the dead chief and drew a cross on de Burgo's shield, saying 'These be thine arms forever.' However, Richard I was not born until 8 September 1157 and only took part in the third crusade in 1189–92. Nevertheless, the de Burgo family was certainly involved in the Crusades.

Merchants' Marks

There is a series of symbols carved on the late medieval stonework of Galway city which are known as merchants' marks. They are sometimes confused with heraldic arms; however, while some appear side by side with coats of arms, heralds frowned upon these carvings. There are at least twenty-two examples in Galway city dating from the late medieval to the early historic period. They were essentially personal identification marks used by all classes of citizens. These marks served a very practical purpose: reproduced on goods, they could easily identify for a mostly illiterate population things belonging to a particular merchant or trader. It is, therefore, difficult to describe a typical merchant's mark as there are so many variations. However, a characteristic merchant's mark was carved within a stone shield or roundel and consisted of a vertical shaft topped with a cross, inverted V, double X or W, the number four symbol, or variations of all of these. The base of the stem could also end in a cross.

Merchants' marks are not unique to Galway, and while their origin is somewhat obscure, it has been suggested that their usage began in continental Europe and spread to Ireland through the normal course of trade. It is not surprising that so many examples are still to be found in Galway as it was such an important trading port.

These symbols were in widespread use in Galway during the fifteenth and sixteenth centuries, but had fallen out of fashion by the late seventeenth century. This is not surprising, as the city fell to the forces of Cromwell midway through that century and many merchants suffered terribly, being forced out of their homes and businesses. Properties were handed over to Cromwellian soldiers who knew little or nothing of maintaining these mansions and even less about trade, which suffered immense damage and never really recovered. Over time the merchants disappeared and their trading marks were all but forgotten.[236]

The Daggered Heart

There is a daggered heart symbol carved into the top of a wall located along Nimmo's Pier in the Claddagh.

---

236 P. Walsh, 'The Medieval Merchants' Mark and its Survival in Galway', *Journal of the Galway Archaeological & Historical Society*, vol. 45, 1993, pp. 1–3.

While there are a small number of similar carvings along the same wall, the daggered heart carving is the best example, the others possibly being later copies. This symbol is a classic design and captures people's attention and emotions. It also seems to have various meanings for different societies and people. In the Christian world, it is said to represent the Catholic Sacred Heart of Mary grieving for her son. Mary is often referred to as the Mother of Sorrows, after Simeon's words to her in the temple: 'A sword shall pierce through thine own soul also.' By contrast, in voodoo the symbol is used to symbolise Erzulie Dantor, goddess of love, romance, art, jealousy and passion, and a fierce defender of women.

Another school of thought attempts to combine the meanings of the two symbols. From earliest times the heart has represented love, and today it is used worldwide as a symbol of romantic love. In contrast to this, the dagger was the stealthy weapon of choice for assassins, since it was easy to conceal. It represented not simply the physical stab wound, but also a sense of betrayal and hurt – the attacker had to be close to the victim. The daggered heart, therefore, essentially represents the heart in great pain. Sometimes this pain is a mortal wound; sometimes a love betrayed; and in some cases a sacrifice made.[237]

The daggered heart symbol carved on the wall of Nimmo's Pier is to some extent a mystery, as the artist is unknown and it is not known when or why it was carved (although it was perhaps sometime in the late nineteenth

---

237 'More Tattoo Symbols and their Symbolism', www.tattoosymbol.com/ articles/heart-dagger.html December 2010.

or early twentieth century). It is believed that the centre of the carving contained a red diamond-type heart many years ago, which has since disappeared. While thousands walk along the pier throughout the year, the existence of the carving is unknown to most people.[238]

Merlin Park Castle

The castle of Merlin Park was also once known as Doughiska Castle. It is not a castle in the strictest sense, but rather a tower house, and is located in the grounds of a former 'gentleman's park' bearing the same name. The tower house-building era in Ireland was from around 1440 to 1640. In 1383 Henry Blake, a member of that famous Galway tribe, leased a section of the lands of Doughiska from Dermot O'Connor, the Abbot of Knockmoy. According to a detailed survey of the castle carried out during the early part of the twentieth century, the area was once the property of James Lynch Fitzstephen, the mayor of Galway, who in 1493 was reputed to have executed his own son for murdering a visiting Spaniard. A local historian, W. J. Burke of Ower, who died in 1895, said that it was common knowledge throughout his lifetime that James Lynch Fitzstephen was at one stage the owner of the castle. While these stories

---

238 Interview: Michael Connelly, 12 May 2010.

cannot be substantiated, the Lynch family did have land in this area at that time, and certainly in Ballybane, today a neighbouring housing estate.

By 1564 Nicholas Fitzjohn Blake was in possession of the land and castle. His daughter, Evelyn, inherited the property. She married into the Lynch family and by 1574 it was the property of Stephen Lynch. They Lynch family lost the land and castle during the Cromwellian confiscations of 1653–5.[239] In 1820 the historian James Hardiman recorded in his list of 'Forfeited Lands in the Liberties of Galway' for 1657 that Michael Lynch lost his property to William Buckley. He also said that Merlin Park Castle was probably 'unroofed' by the Cromwellians. Following the restoration of the monarchy in 1660, John Whaley acquired three-quarters of the lands and castle.[240] He sold the property to Francis Blake in 1680 and in 1731 his grandson, also Francis Blake, is recorded as being the first of this family actually to reside there. It was during his lifetime that the area became known as Merlin Park. It is not known why it was named as such, but there is a tradition that it was named after Merlin from the court of King Arthur of Camelot. Francis Blake died in 1763 and ten years later the castle and lands were sold in the Encumbered Estate Court to M. Hodgson. However, the Blakes did retain a section of the land and built Merlin Park House.

The entire property was later sold to Robert Waithman,

239 Athy and Hodgson, 'Notes on the Ordnance Survey Letters', pp. 146–52.
240 Hardiman, *History of the Town and County*, pp. 162–3.

grandfather of Captain Wyndham Waithman, and the Waithman family lived there until 1945 when the land was acquired by the government to accommodate Merlin Park Hospital.[241] Some restoration work was carried out on the castle in recent years and it was also made safe, as children from the nearby housing estates now play around the structure. It is a fine example of a late medieval tower house.

Italian Madonna of the Rosary

On 22 May 1922 the statue of the Madonna of the Rosary was carried in a great procession of clergy and people through the old village of the Claddagh. It was taken to the local Dominican church, and while the congregation sang and prayed, the Madonna was raised to her place of honour on the gospel side of the high altar. The procession and restoration of the statue was a symbol of the renewal of the Catholic faith and of freedom – the people had at last released themselves from under the heel of the oppressor with the foundation of the Irish state. The statue was now to share in the joy of the people in a new era of honour and respect.[242]

---

241 Athy and Hodgson, 'Notes on the Ordnance Survey Letters', pp. 146–52.

242 'St Mary's On the Hill', *Brat Muire/The Mantle*, no. 51, 1970, pp. 4–5.

This wooden statue is in the baroque style and is possibly of Italian origin. It is believed to have been on display in the earlier church which was built in 1669. A detailed history of the effigy cannot be traced throughout the turbulent years of the seventeenth century and the subsequent Penal Laws.[243] However, it is known that in 1683 John Kirwan and his wife Mary presented a silver crown to the Dominican order that was placed on the head of the statue. The crown carries the following inscription: 'Pray for the souls of John Kirwan and his wife Mary 1683'. In 1686 John Kirwan became the first Catholic mayor of Galway for over thirty years. It has been suggested that the Kirwans actually brought the statue back from Italy and presented it to the church.

Another suggestion is that the Dominicans themselves brought the statue back from either Naples or Rome with the intention of spreading devotion to the rosary. This would seem more likely, given that a confraternity was established during the seventeenth century, with the Dominican church in the Claddagh being the celebrated centre of the rosary. Towards the end of that century, mounting persecution and anti-Catholic feelings forced the Dominicans to vacate their church. In April 1698 the two remaining priests, Prior Gregory Ffrench and Fr Nicholas Blake, would not leave until they had safely packed away the sacred vessels and vestments into a large chest. Among the treasures they stored was the crown. Before leaving they handed the chest over to a close and trusted friend, Valentine Browne, a merchant of the town. They then removed the Madonna

---

243   Ó hEideain, *Dominicans in Galway*, p. 65.

from her niche and are supposed to have placed it in the custody of a Catholic family. However, according to local Dominican tradition, the statue was buried in the priory grounds for safekeeping. It was later retrieved and placed in the church built towards the end of the Penal Laws.

Br Alphonsus O'Donoghue, who was born in 1838, mentions in his notebook that during his lifetime the statue stood on a pedestal inside the priory door, unnoticed for almost a century. It had been damaged and was in need of restoration work. Sometime after the building of the present church in 1891, Fr William Stephens found the statue in a rather neglected state in the priory. He also discovered the notebook and realised the importance of the statue. In 1921 he sent it to Cullen's of Dominick Street in Dublin where restoration work was carried out.[244] Upon completion of the work the statue was returned to Galway, where a grateful people received it. The pearl rosary beads that now adorn the statue were a donation from John Clancy, a Claddagh fisherman. John had brought the beads back from a visit to Jerusalem in 1922 and his mother presented them to the Dominican order.[245] The Madonna is set against a mosaic background depicting kneeling Claddagh fisher folk against a crystal-blue sea and brown sails of the Galway hookers, all under the protection of St Nicholas and St Enda.

The statue is sometimes referred to as Our Lady of Galway. It has survived the ravages of war and persecution, and is a treasured possession in the community. It stands

---

244 'St Mary's on the Hill', pp. 4–5.
245 Ó hEideain, *Dominicans in Galway*, p. 65.

as a clear reminder of the sufferings of people of a bygone age. While numerous people visit this church, not many are aware of importance of the statue or its history.[246]

Charles Ffrench Blake-Forster

C harles Ffrench Blake-Forster was born in Forster House, Forster Street, in 1850 and was said to be blessed with a gifted mind and an outstanding intellect. His father was Captain Francis Blake-Forster of the Connaught Rangers and his mother was Mary Josephine Comerford, the daughter of Henry Comerford, a successful Galway merchant. Young Blake-Forster was aware of his family background and was extremely proud of its history and powerful association with Galway.[247]

The Forster family was originally from Hunsdon, Hertfordshire, in England and had arrived in Galway during the 1640s. Francis Forster was granted the Clooneene/ Ashfield property in County Galway by King Charles II on 18 August 1677. Another property associated with the family was Hermitage House, the residence of Francis Blake-Forster, which has been in ruins since the mid-twentieth

246 'St Mary's on the Hill', p. 4.
247 'Galway of the Tribes: The Irish Chieftains or a Struggle for the Crown', *Galway Advertiser*, 25 January 2001.

century. The family also had houses at Rathorpe and Fiddaun, as well as property in Kilfenora and Drumcreehy in County Clare. Francis Forster, who inherited some of the family estates in 1752, married Anastasia Blake of Menlo, and it was then that the family became known as Blake-Forster.[248] It is not known for certain when they first moved to the residence in College Road in Galway, but it was perhaps sometime in the early nineteenth century.

Charles Ffrench Blake-Forster was first educated at home and later at Stonyhurst College near Birmingham in England. His father had inherited Duras House in Kinvara from his father-in-law, who had acquired it from the de Basterot family sometime after the Great Famine of 1845–50. Upon his return from England, Charles made this his principal residence.[249] While still in his late teens he began playing a prominent role in Galway city's public affairs, becoming a town councillor and a member of the Board of Guardians. In 1874 he presided at three parliamentary elections and was also High Sheriff of Galway, with responsibilities in administering justice and ensuring peace in the city.[250] He presided over the first elections held for members of parliament under a new Ballot Act that had just been introduced. He had been nominated for the East Ward seat of the town council, and the townspeople held him in such high esteem that they went ahead and

248 'Forster (Blake Forster)', www.landedestates.ie/LandedEstates/jsp/estate-show.jsp?id=760 (accessed April 2010).

249 'Galway of the Tribes'.

250 'Charles Ffrench Blakeforster', *Brat Muire/ The Mantle*, no. 47, 1968–1972, p. 32.

elected him to that post posthumously as a mark of respect.

Blake-Forster's contribution to society and his academic genius was just beginning to be recognised when he died of a brain haemorrhage on 9 September 1874 at the age of twenty-four. His obituary declared that the 'great labour he had undergone in his untiring literary pursuits had affected his constitution, and the fatigue and mental anxiety consequent upon the illness and death of a beloved sister proved too much for him to bear'.

Although dying at such a young age, Blake-Forster's achievements were amazing. His literary work included historical articles and essays: 'What are the Arms of Galway?'; 'A Historical and Biographical Memoir of Major General Don Hugh Balldearg O'Donnell'; 'A Historical Sketch of the De Birminghams, Lords of Athenry'; 'The Annals of Athenry'; 'The Annals of Knockmoy Abbey'; 'The Annals of Corcomroe Abbey'; 'Lemenagh Castle, or, a Legend of the Wild Horse'; and 'Kilfenora, Ye City of Ye Crosses'.[251] Many of these articles and essays were written between 1869 and 1871 and submitted to *The Galway Vindicator* and *The Galway Express* newspapers, and they were very well received. His essay on Kilfenora in particular bears testament to his 'sterling patriotism' and dedication to his work. Blake-Forster also studied many ancient books and manuscripts and also interviewed some renowned genealogists of the period.

He had a vast knowledge, which can be seen from his

---

251 'Galway of the Tribes'.

book *The Irish Chieftains, or, a Struggle for the Crown*, an historical study of south Galway and north Clare and an account of the Williamite War in Ireland from a Galway perspective, which was published in 1872 by McGlashran & Gill. While it is described as a novel, it is without doubt an astonishing account of events and individuals mixed with stories from other centuries. Even the notes and appendices that accompany this work form a volume in themselves and are astonishingly detailed.[252] According to a relative, this work caused problems for Blake-Forster among the leading aristocratic families of the day, and he was expelled from the County Clubs of Ennis and Galway for expressing his nationalist opinions. The binding of the manuscript was also decorated with an uncrowned harp, which some found offensive. Blake-Forster had just completed another very important manuscript, *The Annals of Galway*, at the time of his death, but it was subsequently lost, and with its disappearance a vast knowledge of Galway was also gone.[253] It is believed that some ten unpublished manuscripts also disappeared after his death.

Blake-Forster was laid to rest in the family vault at Bushypark on the Galway to Oughterard road. Had he lived to old age, one can only imagine what his contribution to history and his country might have been. Today, Forster Street, Forster Court and Forster House bear his family name, but many people are unaware of the name's origin.

---

252 'Charles Ffrench Blakeforster', p. 32.
253 'Galway of the Tribes'.

The Siege of St Augustine's Fort

While Forthill is associated with the cemetery that occupies the site today, the name derives from a fort that once dominated the town of Galway. Before the fort was built, the Augustinians had an abbey erected on the hill – then known as Abbey Hill – in *c.* 1500. Towards the end of the sixteenth century there were fears of a Spanish invasion and because the hill overlooked the town it was chosen as a military site. The Augustinians were asked to move into the town, where they were given suitable accommodation. In 1600 Lord Deputy Mountjoy ordered the construction of a star-shaped fort. As this was a directive from Queen Elizabeth I, work began immediately. Masons from various parts of the country worked diligently with local craftsmen and the fort was completed in three years. The old Augustinian abbey was also converted into a barracks.

According to historian James Hardiman, writing in 1820, the fort was one of the finest in the realm. It was protected by stone walls over eighteen feet in height and was surrounded by a huge ditch. The defence positions were equipped with four demi-cannons and four whole culverins. The fort commanded a view of the main approaches to the town by land and sea, which made it very imposing. On 28 May 1603 Sir Thomas Rotheram was appointed governor and served for thirty-three years. He was also mayor of Galway in 1612, the only non-tribal mayor up to that time.

The fortification, which became known as St Augustine's Fort, gave a sense of security to the people of the town for many years. However, the civil war between Charles I and the parliament in England had serious effects in Ireland, and in Galway the townspeople generally remained loyal to the king while the troops at St Augustine's Fort sided with parliament. It was inevitable that hostilities would break out between the two sides. They did so in March 1642.

The governor of the fort, Sir Francis Willoughby, was in Dublin at the time and the fort was under the command of his son, Captain Anthony Willoughby. Young Willoughby, being rash and violent by nature, only made matters between the two sides worse.[254] He withheld payments for supplies to the fort, which infuriated the merchants of the city. While there were some divisions among the townspeople regarding parliament and the monarchy, Willoughby failed to recognise or exploit this situation, and showed utter contempt for all the citizens.[255] At one point, Willoughby and his men captured Redmond Burke, a royalist and experienced soldier, along with two of his comrades on their way into the town. He had them taken to the fort where he bound and hanged them in full view of the townspeople.[256]

The Earl of Clanricarde was governor of the town and county and had on a number of occasions intervened in a bid to prevent further violence. However, he was losing control and popularity to the clergy in the town, who were in favour

---

254 Hardiman, *History of the Town and County*, pp. 96–8.

255 O'Sullivan, *Old Galway*, p. 237.

256 Hardiman, *History of the Town and County*, pp. 96–8.

of besieging the fort and starving the parliamentarians into submission.[257]

On 7 August 1642 the parliamentarian commander, Alexander Lord Forbes, and his fleet of seventeen ships sailed into Galway Bay to support Captain Willoughby. Forbes had his cannon placed in the grounds of the Dominican church in the Claddagh and as a warning of what would happen if Galway did not surrender he burned some of the surrounding villages. Having failed in his bid to lift the siege and force Galway to surrender, Forbes sailed away on 4 September. However, before doing so, he had the Claddagh church defaced and ordered his men to dig up the graves in the cemetery. They then burned the coffins and the remains of the corpses as a final insult.

Hostilities between the fort and town continued after Forbes departed. In one incident, soldiers from the fort managed to slip past the besieging troops and raid and kill a number of innocent men, women and children. Later a Captain Constable stood on the ramparts of the fort and shouted a warning to the townspeople of the consequences for being in opposition to parliament, saying, 'A new king, you rogues and traitors; your king is run away; you will have a new king shortly, you rogues!'[258]

Willoughby's reckless nature further added to the problems. In the early months of 1643 he began firing his cannon into the town. The troops in the town reacted by

---

257 P. Walsh, 'Rinmore Fort: A Seventeenth-Century Fortification at Renmore, Galway', *Journal of the Galway Archaeological & Historical Society* , vol. 41, 1987–1988, p. 120.

258 Hardiman, *History of the Town and County*, pp. 116–18.

fortifying two strategic positions: one fort was erected at Rintinane point, approximately where Nimmo's Pier is today, the other was erected at Renmore, behind the present military barracks (part of this fortification still exists). It was hoped that they would be able to control any shipping coming into the port, and to ensure this they had a chain or 'boom' drawn across the harbour to stop vessels approaching.

The admiral of the fleet appointed to guard the Irish coast was ordered by parliament to proceed to Galway. He sent Captain William Brooke to Galway Bay to assess the situation, but as his ship approached the harbour it was fired upon from the two new fortifications. Brooke attempted to send in smaller vessels under cover of darkness, but these were also repulsed.[259] The royalists had now taken control, and with St Augustine's Fort sealed off by land and sea there was little hope of the siege being lifted. The town troops also put cannons in place to fire on the parliamentarians. The citizens of Galway had now nailed their colours to the mast and had taken the oath of union, swearing allegiance to King Charles I, a decision for which they later suffered.[260]

Colonel John Burke, a distinguished soldier, arrived in Galway to take command of the town garrison. He had been appointed lieutenant-general of Connacht in October 1642 by the General Assembly of Catholics in Kilkenny.[261] His military experience changed the situation, and following the failure of Captain Brooke and his fleet to relieve the

259 Walsh, 'Rinmore Fort: A Seventeenth-Century Fortification at Renmore, Galway', p. 120.
260 O'Sullivan, *Old Galway*, pp. 240, 245.
261 O'Dowd, *Old and New Galway*, p. 27.

fort, Willoughby knew that his days were numbered. On 20 June 1643 he requested that terms of surrender be drawn up. These were agreed, and on 25 June Willoughby and his men were given safe passage to board the parliamentarian ships awaiting them in the bay. The town rejoiced, almost excessively, with public prayers of thanksgiving being offered throughout the city.

The fort that had dominated the Galway skyline for over forty years was soon demolished.[262] Part of its foundations were exposed some years ago when work was being carried out at the cemetery, but all that remains of its existence today is the name Forthill.

Anti-Courting Devices

Protecting the alcoves or corner sections on the façade of what was commonly known as Fr Daly's chapel in Newtownsmith are a number of iron bars. These bars are spiked and curved and are strategically placed so access cannot be gained to the alcoves of the building. Most people pass these on a daily basis without even noticing them. Those who do often wonder about their purpose. According to local tradition in Galway they were put there to prevent courting couples from utilising these alcoves and

---

262   Hardiman, *History of the Town and County*, pp. 121–2.

corner areas, hence the term 'anti-courting devices'. The older people would tell you that it saved the priest chasing couples away with a stick. They can be found for the most part on nineteenth-century buildings in many towns and cities throughout Ireland.[263]

Mount St Mary

When Dr Francis MacCormack was appointed bishop of Galway in 1887 there was no official residence. Bishop George Browne had lived at Maryville, Newcastle; Laurence O'Donnell in Fort Lorenzo; John McEvilly in Prospect Hill; and Thomas Carr had lived at Murrough. Dr MacCormack set about looking for a suitable residence and purchased a house at Taylor's Hill, called Mount Vernon, for £1,500. The name of the residence was later changed to Mount St Mary, but it was more commonly known as the Bishop's Palace.

The house was originally the home of Thomas Moore Persse, a corn merchant, who leased the site from a local priest, Fr Peter Daly, on 18 May 1860.[264] Having spent his early years in the United States, Persse was influenced

263 W. Henry, 'Hidden Galway', lecture to the Old Galway Society, 3 March 2005.
264 His nephew, Burton Persse, owned the whiskey distillery at Newcastle.

by American architecture and had all the timber for the building of the house imported from Virginia. He was also an admirer of the founding fathers of the United States, hence the original name of Mount Vernon, after George Washington's home in Virginia. Sometime between 1880 and 1885 he had a painting of the house commissioned. The artist, Colonel Frank Knatchbull, was related to him through marriage. The painting later formed part of a private Persse family collection in Canada.

Thomas Persse was a benevolent man who was very generous to local charities and gained much respect from the public. A highly respected borough magistrate, he sat on all the public boards and was chairman of the town commissioners for several years. During his time the town gained its new waterworks system, which was greatly welcomed by the public. It seems that Thomas Persse invested large sums of his own money in relief committees in a bid to try to improve conditions for the poor. However, by 1874 he had run into financial difficulties and was forced to sell Mount Vernon to Redmond Burke. Eight years later, in 1882, William Morris Reade purchased the estate through the high court. Following his death, his wife, Almeria Jane Reade, sold the house to Dr MacCormack and it was the official residence of the bishops of Galway until recent times. Thomas Moore Persse died in 1884, aged seventy-five, and is buried in the New Cemetery, Bohermore.[265]

---

265 T. M. May, 'Mount St Mary's and Thomas Moore Persse', *Diocese of Galway Directory*, May 1994, pp. 87–9.

The Empty Picture Frame

Located on the end wall in the south transept of St Nicholas' Collegiate Church is a square stone fixture known as the 'empty picture frame'. For many years it has been associated with a painting of the Madonna and Child that according to tradition once adorned the picture frame.

There is a painting of the Blessed Virgin holding the child Jesus in her arms in the cathedral of Gyor in Hungary called *Consolatrix Afflictorum*. In English, it is known as 'Our Lady of Consolation', or 'Comforter of the Afflicted'. According to tradition, this painting was removed from St Nicholas' Collegiate Church in Galway and taken to Gyor by Rev. Walter Lynch in 1655. Lynch was at one time a warden in the church of St Nicholas and later bishop of Clonfert and was reputed to have taken the painting to protect it from the Cromwellians, who had entered the city in 1652. Following Lynch's death in July 1663, the painting was placed in the cathedral in Gyor. On 17 March 1697 it was reported that the Blessed Virgin began to weep 'copiously' before a large number of people. It was also reported that the image exuded a 'bloody sweat' for some three hours.

It was 200 years before people in Ireland became aware of the miracle associated with the painting. In 1863 the bishop of Gyor had restoration work carried out on it and in a pastoral letter he gave the following information:

An outstanding and venerable respect accrues to this church from the sacred image of the Blessed Virgin which Walter Lynch, sometime bishop of Clonfert, brought with him from Ireland and regarded with particular devotion. When the followers of Cromwell were fiercely raging against Catholicism, he had been compelled to exchange his native place for exile, and in the year 1655 had been admitted a member of the college of canons in Gyor. He passed away in 1663. Because of the repute of his esteemed piety and singular virtue, the painting was hung on the wall of the church at the back of the altar of St Anne.[266]

The story from an Irish context was first recorded in 1897 by Fr James Ryan, vice-president of St Patrick's College in Thurles. He had been on a visit to Hungary when he was made aware of the story. He published his article in the *Irish Ecclesiastical Record* and since then a number of other articles on the subject have appeared in various journals and papers. There was also a film produced of the 'sweating of blood' for the 250th anniversary of the famous event in Gyor. The film was shown in Galway, and following its screening more people became aware of the story, resulting in a deepening of the tradition. However, it also prompted more serious investigations by a number of people and an association was made with the painting and the empty picture frame, perhaps because Rev. Lynch was once a warden of St Nicholas' Church. However, the connection of the 'Weeping Madonna', as she became known in Galway, with the empty picture frame cannot be validated.

---

266 J. Mitchell, 'Fiction and "The Empty Picture Frame": Gyor and Galway', *Journal of the Galway Archaeological & Historical Society* vol. 40, 1985–6, pp. 20, 23.

There is a tomb located just beneath the frame that is associated with the Lynch family, one of the most influential and powerful tribes of Galway. (The south aisle of the church is also called the Lynch aisle.) At least one source states that the frame was 'clearly designed' to accompany the tomb by housing a plaque of some kind to commemorate the person or persons interred therein. It is also clear that at the time when the painting was supposed to have been removed from the church Walter Lynch was not the warden: Dr Patrick Lynch had succeeded him, so Walter would not have had the authority to take the painting. There is always the possibility that he was granted permission to remove the painting. However, it has been suggested that this was highly unlikely given that the overwhelming majority of clergy and townspeople were against the surrender of Galway to the Cromwellians. While most sources indicate that Walter Lynch brought the painting to Gyor from Ireland, there is no real evidence to indicate that the painting was ever in St Nicholas' Church. Nevertheless, it has become part of a tradition in Galway, and indeed Gyor, that will not be displaced by historical facts.

The painting has been described as being on canvas, 26 inches in height and 20 inches in width. However, the artist, and indeed the school of painting to which it belongs, is unknown. A professional art critic suggested that it was possibly a seventeenth-century painting of Italian origin. Another expert suggested that it was from a Flemish school in the style of Pieter Pourbus of Bruges; another indicates that it may be of Spanish origin, probably from the school of Velazquez and Murillo. While many historians would not agree with the tradition of the painting in connection to the empty picture frame in Galway, some would agree that there is a possibility that the Lynch family had it commissioned for the church.

In the 1980s a copy of the 'Weeping Madonna' was placed in the empty picture frame and the picture was clearly smaller than the space reserved for it. However, it was later removed, leaving the picture frame empty again. Its conspicuous absence added to the tradition. Today, an image of St Nicholas adorns the 'empty picture frame'.[267]

The Gashouse

The Galway Gas Company opened at some point before or during the Great Famine of 1845–50. We know this because in 1846 a 'notice', a warning, was posted on the wall of the gashouse to the town commissioners concerning the export of food from the port while people were starving.[268] While some sources indicate that it was officially opened in 1869, the 'notice' seems to contradict this date: however, it could have been posted on an earlier building.

The gashouse, as it was known, was situated in Queen Street. The fuel used to produce the gas was called 'gas coal'

---

267 *Ibid.*, pp. 24, 25, 28, 34, 38, 39, 47.
268 'Notice', *The Galway Mercury*, 24 January 1846.

and was a special type of coal imported from England. The stokers fed the retort house from a huge coal shed, and the coal was burned at the extremely high temperatures required to extract the gas. When the coal was burned and the gas removed, one of the extracts that remained was a black residue, which resembled coal, known as coke, and was used by convents, bakeries and indeed houses all around the town for heating and cooking. Another residue from this process was a liquid tar that was used for 'tarring' the roofs of sheds and outhouses – this was a time of little or no waste; everything was used. People from all over the town went to the gashouse to purchase bags of coal dust, which they would dampen and form into round shapes known as 'duff'. This was a cheap form of fuel that was also used for heating and cooking, as it burned for long periods.

The structure where the gas was stored was known as the gasometer. As the gas was produced, the sides of the gasometer rose to show how much gas was available. There was always two feet of water at the base of the gasometer to stop the gas escaping into the ground. The height of the gasometer above the ground was the same as below ground, depending on the amount of gas being stored.

By the mid-twentieth century most people in the city had gas meters installed in their homes and some factories were also fitted with them. When people wanted to use the gas, they put money in the meter. It has been estimated that it took about three old pennies to boil a kettle of water. The house meters were emptied every six weeks and the factory meters every month. The money was collected in a 'money cart', which resembled a hand cart and was wheeled about town by two gashouse employees. While there was much poverty at that time, there was little crime, so the employees and the cart of coins were safe, indicating a respect for law and order. Some houses paid for the gas directly and children could be seen making their way to the gashouse with the money wrapped in a piece of brown paper to pay the bill for their parents. Shift work was required to keep up gas production and people were delighted with the employment.

The Galway Gas Company also had a shop in Mainguard Street. It sold many items such as gas cookers, gas fires and even a gas dryer for clothes, plus another item called a gas water heater. The gashouse closed on 28 October 1968 after ninety-nine years of supplying gas to the homes of Galway.[269] All that remains of it now is a fine stone gateway facing Galway docks, which many people today enquire about. It is incredible how quickly this part of everyday life was forgotten and confined to hidden history.

The Roscam Standing Stone

The Roscam standing stone is located close to an old monastic site overlooking Galway Bay. It is very distinctive, being 2.45 metres high, and there are possibly

---

269 C. Thornton, 'The Galway Gas House', *St Patrick's Parish Magazine*, 2008, p. 34.

the remains of a Bronze Age burial, known as a cist grave, at its base. The monument is now difficult to access because of development and is hidden away from view.

Folklore and the ancient *Annals of Ulster* tell us that the stone was erected in memory of the Abbot of Roscam, who was killed on this spot during the Battle of Connacht, which took place in AD 835. However, Muriel Athy Lynch, writing for the *Galway Archaeological and Historical Journal* in 1913–14, informs us that the *Annals of Connacht* record that this stone was erected by St Hugh of Roscam over the grave of the great King Brian, the ancestor of all the kings of Connacht of the Hy Brian race. The O'Connor, O'Flaherty and O'Rourke clans can all trace their ancestry to him. King Brian was the older brother of Niall of the Nine Hostages, the first *ard rí* [high king] of Ireland, and his sons were supposed to have been baptised by St Patrick himself. According to tradition, St Patrick was first brought to Ireland from Wales, having been captured by a band of Irish warriors led by Niall of the Nine Hostages.[270]

We are very fortunate in Ireland to have so many surviving stone monuments. Of these, the standing stone is the simplest type found. The Irish term used for these monuments is *gallan* or *dallan*. The stones vary in height from less than a metre to over 6 metres, the tallest example being located at Punchestown in County Kildare. The purpose of standing stones is somewhat puzzling. Some archaeologists believe they marked the site of a grave, and

---

270 Athy and Hodgson, 'Notes on the Ordnance Survey Letters', pp. 164–5.

some excavated examples have indeed produced short cist graves, which have been dated to the early Bronze Age, *c.* 2000 BC. A cist grave is constructed with flat stone slabs lining four sides. One flat stone is then laid along the bottom and another on top, thus forming a box-shaped grave set into the ground. The average measurements of the short graves were about 80 cm long by 50 cm wide and 50 cm deep. Both cremation and inhumation burials were practised during this period. In the case of the unburned short cist burial, the body was placed on its side with the knees drawn up to the chin, possibly tied in that position, and then placed in the grave. This type of burial is often referred to as a crouched burial. A single pot – presumably a food vessel containing an offering of food or drink for the deceased spirit – was sometimes placed beside the head of the corpse. However, no conclusive evidence has survived to show the exact function of these pots.[271]

Other standing stones cannot be so easily explained and it has been suggested they could have been markers along prehistoric trackways. There were, up to recent times, the remains of an old road or trackway that presumably led to the monastery at Roscam. It is possible that this road could have developed along an ancient trackway over time? Given that the standing stone at Roscam marks a short cist grave, the question remains: did it also indicate an ancient trackway in this area?

Estyn Evens, who has carried out extensive field survey

---

271 M. J. O'Kelly, *Early Ireland: An Introduction to Irish Prehistory* (Cambridge: Cambridge University Press, 1989), p. 189.

work throughout the country, has suggested that some stones were erected as late as the last century as scratching posts for cattle and that perhaps many of the 'true' early examples survived because of this. However, Roscam is a genuine standing stone that has its origins in Ireland's prehistory.[272]

Rory Murtagh

Rory Murtagh, an adventurer and soldier, was born in Galway in 1752, when the anti-Catholic Penal Laws were being enforced. Galway was under the control of a Protestant ascendancy class who were very loyal to the king. This is borne out by the fact that on 14 December 1752 John Hamlin, the mayor of Galway, and his corporation drafted a letter to King George II to congratulate him on his safe return to the British dominions after a visit to France. The letter also pledged the town's loyalty and expressed the joy felt by all on His Majesty's safe return, 'which we consider as the greatest blessing to all your subjects'.[273] It is important to note these factors, as they may well have influenced Rory Murtagh's decisions as an adult.

272 P. Harbison, *Pre-Christian Ireland: From the First Settlers to the Early Celts* (London: Thames and Hudson, 1988), p. 96.
273 Henry, *Role of Honour*, p. 107.

As a youth in the city, Murtagh earned a reputation as a daredevil. At the tender age of ten he allowed himself to be rolled down the main street of the town in a blazing barrel for a bet of two pence. Little is known of his parents, but upon leaving school at the age of twelve he became an apprentice to a blacksmith named Seamus O'Grady. In time, Murtagh became renowned for his strength and skill. He earned the respect of his employer and when O'Grady died, ownership of the forge passed to Murtagh. Even as a young man, he never lost his love of a challenge, and it seems that his summer evenings were spent accepting all sorts of formidable tasks, much to the amusement of the locals.[274]

By 1774 tension was growing between the American colonists and the British. Matters worsened after Patrick Henry, lawyer and revolutionary, sounded his rallying cry: 'I know not what course others may take, but as for me, give me liberty or give me death!'[275] As the situation deteriorated many businesses in the colonies, England and Ireland were finding it difficult to survive. Even Galway was affected by the political situation that had developed and it seems that Murtagh was forced out of business. This may not be the full reason for him shutting down his forge, but he immediately joined the army of King George III and after some initial training found himself on the way to the war in America. However, like other Irishmen, Murtagh's true sympathies lay with the colonists.

---

274   L. Bowes, 'Rory Murtagh of Galway', *Ireland's Own*, 1992.

275   'The First Continental Congress', *The World Book Encyclopaedia* (1986).

Some weeks after arriving in America, he and six others failed to answer the regimental roll call one morning and a search ensued. By this time Murtagh and the others were on the way to Concord to join Paul Revere's radicals.[276] On 18 April 1775, 700 British troops marched out from Boston to seize the military stores at Concord and arrest two of the colonial leaders, Samuel Adams and John Hancock. However, Paul Revere and William Dawes rode ahead and warned the rebels of the British advance. At Lexington Green a thin line of armed 'minutemen' tried to stop the soldiers, but failed. The British marched on to Concord, where they destroyed the colonists' supplies.[277]

However, the British made the mistake of staying too long at Concord. The shots fired by the radicals at Lexington and Revere's warnings had the desired effect, bringing out a huge number of colonists. According to one source, Rory Murtagh was in the front line of revolutionaries, calling out, amongst other things, 'Revenge for Ireland!'[278] In the engagement that followed, the British were forced to retreat.

The signing of the Declaration of Independence on 4 July 1776 by the American colonists set the path for all-out war between the now fledging country and Great Britain.[279] Murtagh remained with the American revolutionaries throughout the war, taking part in a number of bloody actions and earning the respect of all who fought with him.

276 Bowes, 'Rory Murtagh'.

277 'Concord, Battle of', *The World Book Encyclopaedia* (1986).

278 Bowes, 'Rory Murtagh'.

279 A. Cooke, *Alistair Cooke's America* (London: Book Club Associates, 1981), pp. 107, 120.

He gained great knowledge of his adopted country and later worked as a trail-scout with a wagon train, which led him into a number of clashes with the native Sioux. This was followed by a career with a travelling circus, where he was billed as 'Red Rory – the Man Who Laughs at Death'. His risky escapades as a youth in Galway certainly came in useful: during one of his performances he was mauled by a grizzly bear, and in another he simulated being hanged by the neck. It seems that he had powerful neck muscles and could tense himself to such a degree that he was able to withstand strangulation for several minutes, thus astonishing the crowd. It is believed that in 1796 he walked backwards from Texas to Missouri for $500. He never returned to Galway and died in October 1819 from severe burns received when his home was destroyed by fire.[280]

Emily Anderson

The story of Emily Anderson is fascinating and was only revealed when research for an academic history of University College Galway for the university's 160th anniversary in 2009 was carried out. Emily was the daughter of Alexander Anderson, Professor of Physics and President of University College from 1899 until 1934. Her

---

280 Bowes, 'Rory Murtagh'.

mother was Emily Binns from Galway. The Andersons had four children, three daughters and a son, and Emily was born in March 1891. The family lived in the quadrangle building in the college and Emily was educated privately before taking up her studies at University College Galway. In 1909 she received first place and first-class honours in English, German, French and Latin, which won her a literary scholarship. She almost repeated this performance in her second year, was the Browne scholar for 1909–1910 and took her BA degree in 1911. Emily then travelled to Europe, where she undertook two further years of study at the universities of Berlin and Marburg. On returning to Galway, she became an active supporter of women's rights, joining the women's suffrage movement. In January 1913 she became a founder member of the Connacht Women's Franchise League.

By 1915 Emily was teaching at Queen's College, Barbados, a free school for girls founded in 1883. She spent two years there and returned to Galway in 1917 to take up a post in University College Galway as the first professor of German. A year later she radically revised the German programme in the college, prescribing additional literary texts at all levels, with a special emphasis on a theoretical knowledge of German phonetics. She introduced the study of Middle and Old High German and expanded courses on German literature in the eighteenth and nineteenth centuries. Emily resigned from her professorship in 1920, leaving this revised course of study as her legacy to the university. The specific reasons for her resignation are unknown, but it may have been a longing to travel. At the time, student numbers in arts and languages were exceptionally low and she may well have found her work unchallenging. Following her resignation she moved to London and immediately secured a position with the Foreign Office, remaining there for many years.

In 1923 Emily published a translation of a book by Benedetto Croce – the Italian critic, idealist philosopher and occasional politician – on Johann Wolfgang von Goethe. Between 1940 and 1943 she worked for the British War Office and later received the OBE for intelligence which resulted from her work in the Middle East. She retired from the foreign office in 1951 after a distinguished career and devoted the remainder of her life to the academic study of music. Emily had already achieved international distinction in 1938 for her publication of *The Letters of Mozart and his Family*, a work in three volumes, which she edited and translated herself. In 1961, her *Letters of Beethoven*, also in three volumes, were published, having taken some fifteen years to complete. She was awarded the Order of Merit by the Federal Republic of Germany for this work.

Emily died at Hampstead in London in October 1962. In her will she provided for the setting up of an international prize for the violin through the support of the Royal Philharmonic Society.[281]

---

281 'The Remarkable Story of Emily Anderson', *Galway Advertiser*, 8 February 2001.

Bibliography

Books

Andre, S. and Fleischer, N., *A Pictorial History of Boxing* (London: Hamlyn, 1985)

Barry, M., *An Affair of Honour* (Fermoy: Eigse, 1981)

Boylan, H., *Theobald Wolfe Tone* (Dublin: Gill & Macmillan, 1981)

Castleden, R., *British History: A Chronological Dictionary of Dates* (London: Parragon, 1994)

Cheshire, P., *Kings and Queens* (London: Star Fire, 2001)

Cooke, A., *Alistair Cooke's America* (London: Book Club Associates, 1981)

Crealey, A. H., *An Irish Almanac* (Cork: Mercier Press, 1993)

Doherty, R. and Truesdale, D., *Irish Winners of the Victoria Cross* (Dublin: Four Courts Press, 1993)

Fox, E., Leonard, M. and O'Dowd, P., *Introduction to Burrenology* (Galway: Regional Technical College, 1978)

Furey, B., *The History of Oranmore Maree* (Galway: Brenda Furey, 1991)

Gantz, I., *Signpost to Eyrecourt: Portrait of the Eyre Family Triumphant in the Cause of Liberty, Derbyshire, Wiltshire, Galway, c. 1415–1856* (Bath: Kingsmead Press, 1975)

Glover, M., *Warfare from Waterloo to Mons* (London: Cassell, 1980)

Gosling, P., *Archaeological Inventory of County Galway, Volume 1: West Galway* (Dublin: The Stationery Office, 1993)

Harbison, P., *Pre-Christian Ireland: From the First Settlers to the Early Celts* (London: Thames and Hudson, 1988)

Hardiman, J., *The History of the Town and County of the town of*

Galway (Galway: facsimile of 1820 edition, *The Connacht Tribune*, 1985)

Hayward, R., *The Corrib Country* (Dundalk: Dundalgan Press, 1968)

Henry, W., *The Shimmering Waste: The Life and Times of Robert O'Hara Burke* (Galway: William Henry, 1997)

—— *The James Joyce Story and his Galway Connection* (Galway: Merv Griffin, 1999)

—— *St Clerans: The Tale of a Manor House* (Galway: Merv Griffin, 1999)

—— *Role of Honour: The Mayors of Galway City 1485–2001* (Galway: Galway City Council, 2001)

—— *Supreme Sacrifice: The Story of Éamonn Ceannt 1881–1916* (Cork: Mercier Press, 2005)

Higgins, J., *Christian Symbolism and Iconography in Ireland* (forthcoming)

Lynam, S., *Humanity Dick Martin: 'King of Connemara' 1754–1834* (Dublin: The Lilliput Press, 1989)

Maher, H., *Galway Authors* (Galway: Galway County Libraries, 1976)

Montague, H. P., *The Saints and Martyrs of Ireland* (Buckinghamshire: Colin Smythe, 1981)

Murray, J. P., *Galway: A Medico-Social History* (Galway: Kenny's Bookshop & Art Gallery, 1994)

Naughton, M., *The History of St Francis Parish* (Mary Naughton, undated)

Ó hEideain, E., *The Dominicans in Galway 1241–1991* (Galway: The Dominican Priory, 1991)

O'Dowd, P., *Old and New Galway* (Galway: The Archaeological, Historical & Folklore Society and *The Connacht Tribune*, 1985)

—— *St Bridget's Terrace 1912–1987* (St Bridget's Terrace Residents Association, 1987)

—— *Down by the Claddagh* (Galway: Kenny's Bookshop and Art Galleries, 1993)

—— *Galway City* (Galway: Galway Corporation, 1998)

O'Flaherty, R. (edited by J. Hardiman), *A Chorographical Description of West or H-Iar Connaught, Galway 1684* (Dublin: The Irish Archaeological Society, 1846)

O'Kelly, M. J., *Early Ireland: An Introduction to Irish Prehistory* (Cambridge: Cambridge University Press, 1989)

O'Laoi, P., *Nora Barnacle Joyce: A Portrait* (Galway: Kenny's Bookshops, 1982)

—— *History of Castlegar Parish* (Fr Padraic O'Laoi, 1998)

O'Sullivan, M. D., *Old Galway* (Galway: Facsimile reproduction, Kenny's Bookshop & Art Galleries, 1983)

Owen, R., *Great Explorers* (London: Peerage, 1979)

Semple, M., *Reflections on Lough Corrib* (Maurice Semple, 1974)

Sheerin, N., *Renmore and its Environs: A Historical Perspective: Long Live Yesterday* (Galway: Renmore Residents Association, 2000)

Shiel, M. and Roche, D. (eds), *A Forgotten Campaign and Aspects of the Heritage of South-East Galway* (Galway: East Galway Centenary Group, Woodford Heritage Group, 1986)

Villiers-Tuthill, K., *Beyond the Twelve Bens* (Kathleen Villiers-Tuthill, 1990)

Waldron, J., *Maamtrasna* (Dublin: Edmund Burke, 1992)

Walsh, P., *Discover Galway* (Dublin: O'Brien Press, 2001)

General sources

Ceannt, É., 'The Irish Piper: Is He Passing', *Cumann na Píobairí*, Dublin, 1906

Henry, W., 'Lime Kiln', Archaeological Survey, County Galway, 1993

—— 'Tour of Roscam', Tour Leaflet, Galway, 1995

—— 'History of Galway Pubs', Information Leaflet, 2001

—— 'The O'Flaherty Rent', Information Leaflet, Galway, 2010

O'Dowd, P., 'Walking Tour of Old Galway', City Tour Leaflet, Galway, 1 March 1992

Sheerin, N., 'Ancient Graves in Merlin Park', *Frankly Speaking,* Western Health Board Newsletter, Galway, 2002

Interviews

Michael Connelly, 12 May 2010
Jack Small, 10 October 2010
Tom Small, 20 May 2006

Journals

Athy, M. L. and Hodgson, H., 'Notes on the Ordnance Survey Letters', *Journal of the Galway Archaeological & Historical Society*, vol. 8, no. 3, 1913–14

Canny, N., 'Remembering Columbus 1492–1992', *Journal of the Galway Archaeological & Historical Society*, vol. 44, 1992

Collins, T., 'The Town Hall in 1857 – When Galway Hospitality Met Crimean Cannon', *Journal of the Galway Archaeological & Historical Society*, vol. 48, 1996

Dolley, M., 'A Seventeenth-Century Coin-Find from Galway City', *Journal of the Galway Archaeological & Historical Society*, vol. 31, 1964–5

McGuire, S., 'Galway and the Irish Volunteers', *Galway Reader*, vol. 2, nos 1, 2, 1949–50

—— 'Ballinasloe – The Flogging Parson: Honourable and Venerable Charles Le Poer Trench, Archdeacon of Ardagh', *Galway Reader*, vol. 3, nos 1, 2, 1950

—— 'The County Infirmary', *Galway Reader*, vol. 3, nos 1, 2, 1950

—— 'Law and Order in Galway', *Galway Reader*, vol. 4, nos 2, 3, 1954

Mitchell, J., 'The Prisons of Galway: Background to the Inspector General's Reports, 1796–1818', *Journal of the Galway Archaeological & Historical Society*, vol. 49, 1997

—— 'Fiction and "The Empty Picture Frame": Gyor and Galway', *Journal of the Galway Archaeological & Historical Society*, vol. 40, 1985–6

O'Connell, J. 'The Bodkin Murders', *Galway Reader*, vol. 4, no. 1, 1953

O'Dowd, P., 'James Joyce's "The Dead" and its Galway Connections', *Journal of the Galway Archaeological & Historical Society*, vol. 51, 1999

—— 'On Roads and Milestones in County Galway', *Journal of the Galway Archaeological & Historical Society*, vol. 53, 2001

Purcell, C., 'The Armada: How the Spanish Armada Fell upon the West Coast of Ireland A.D. 1588 – Part 1', *Journal of the Westport Historical Society, Cathair na Mart*, vol. 4, no. 1, 1984

Scanlan, B., 'Lighthouses – A Different Perspective', *Journal of the Galway Family History Society: Galway Roots - Clanna na Gaillimhe*, vol. 2, 1994

Walsh, P., 'Rinmore Fort: A Seventeenth-Century Fortification at Renmore, Galway', *Journal of the Galway Archaeological & Historical Society*, vol. 41, 1987–1988

—— 'The Medieval Merchants' Mark and its Survival in Galway', *Journal of the Galway Archaeological & Historical Society*, vol. 45, 1993

Wilkins, D. C. A., 'Defence Prepared: The Galway Militia from 1793', *Journal of the Galway Archaeological & Historical Society*, vol. 50, 1998

Lectures

Claffey, T., 'The Bodkin Murders' (Old Galway Society), 10 October 1996

Henry, W., 'Hidden Galway' (Old Galway Society), 3 March 2005

O'Dowd, P., 'The History of Galway' (Galway Archaeological & Historical Society), 12 June 1993

O'Neill, T. P., 'Christopher Columbus' (Old Galway Society), 12
    October 1992

Magazine articles

'The Augustinians of Abbey Hill or Forthill, Galway', *Brat Muire/
    The Mantle*, no. 46, 1969
'The Black Death: Scourge of Medieval Europe', *Awake*, 8 February
    2000
'Blessed Oliver Plunkett', *Brat Muire/The Mantle*, no. 2, 1958
Bowes, L., 'When Ireland's Meanest Man Became M.P. For
    Galway', *Ireland's Own*, August 1991
—— 'Rory Murtagh of Galway', *Ireland's Own*, October 1992
'Charles Ffrench Blakeforster', *Brat Muire/The Mantle*, no. 47,
    1968–1972
'A Christmas Morning Tragedy', *Brat Muire/The Mantle*, no. 28,
    1964
Editor, 'The Night of the Big Wind', *Ireland's Own*, 15 January 1999
Geoghegan, B. A., 'St Augustine's Holy Well', *Renmore Seagull*, vol.
    3, no. 2, May 1998
Henry, W., 'Bollingbrook Fort', *St Patrick's Parish Magazine*, 1996
—— 'The Cannons at Eyre Square', *St Patrick's Parish Magazine*, 1997
—— 'Mile Stones at Roscam', *St Patrick's Parish Magazine* 2001
—— 'Cooper's Cave', *St Patrick's Parish Magazine*, 2010
—— 'The Justice Stone', *St Patrick's Parish Magazine*, 2010
—— 'The Railway Children', *St Patrick's Parish Magazine*, 2010
May, T. M., 'Mount St Mary's and Thomas Moore Persse', *Diocese
    of Galway Directory*, May 1994
'The Night of the Big Wind', *Brat Muire/The Mantle*, no. 55–6,
    1971
'Pipers' Club Concert', *An Piobaire*, vol. 6, no. 4, September 2010
Sheerin, N., 'The Short Life of Mary McManus', *Renmore Seagull*,
    vol. 15, no. 3, December 2010

'St Mary's On the Hill', *Brat Muire/The Mantle*, no. 51, 1970

'Thomas Nicholas Burke (1830–1883)', *Galway: Official Guide to City and County*, 1986

Thornton, C., 'The Galway Gas House', *St Patrick's Parish Magazine*, 2008

Witington, P., 'Keepers of the Flame', *Cara* (Aer Lingus), vol. 28, no. 6, November–December 1995

Newspaper articles

'Air Disaster Remains Will Arrive in Galway', *The Connacht Tribune*, 16 August 1958

'Another Triumph for Galway Whiskey', *The Galway Vindicator*, 14 December 1898

'Appalling Fire at Menlo Castle', *The Connacht Tribune*, 30 July 1910

'The Ballplaying Nuisance', *The Galway Vindicator*, 29 April 1854

'The Castle to be Rebuilt', *The Connacht Tribune*, 6 August 1910

'The City of the Tribes', *The Connacht Tribune*, 31 December 1910

'Colourful Scenes at Renmore Races', *The Connacht Tribune*, 15 June 1957

'Death of Thomas Ashe', *The Galway Observer*, 11 June 1892

'Execution for Murder', *The Galway Vindicator*, 27 August 1853

'Eyre Square: Monuments and Markets', *Galway Independent*, 10 February 2010

'The Fire at Menlo Castle', *Galway Advertiser*, 9 July 2009

'Galway of the Tribes; The Irish Chieftains or a Struggle for the Crown', *Galway Advertiser*, 25 January 2001

'A Galway V.C.', *The Connacht Tribune*, 9 October 1915

'The Girl who was Carried on a Door', *Galway Advertiser*, 8 March 2007

'The Influenza', *The Galway Express*, 6 January 1900

'Inquest and Funeral of the Air Crash Victims', *The Connacht Tribune*, 23 August 1958

'An Irish Company in the War of 1870–71', *The Tuam Herald*, 16 October 1915

'Island and Sea Service', *The Connacht Tribune*, 23 August 1958

'The Light on Mutton Island', *Galway Advertiser*, 9 June 1994

'Magnificent Repeal Demonstration in Galway', *The Galway Vindicator*, 28 June 1843

'Most Deplorable Accident – Nineteen Persons Drowned!!!', *The Galway Weekly Advertiser and Connaught Journal*, 6 September 1828

'A Note in the Margin', *Galway Advertiser*, 2 November 1992

'Notice', *The Galway Mercury*, 24 January 1846

'Nun's Island Whiskey', *Galway Advertiser*, 6 August 2009

'Objectors in Ruins over Menlo Restoration Project', *Galway Advertiser*, 27 July 2000

'Old Galway', *Galway Advertiser*, 31 January 1985

'The Old Galway', *Galway Advertiser*, 14 December 1995

'Oranmore', *The Connacht Tribune*, 15 October 1921

'Persse's Galway Whiskey', *Galway Advertiser*, 9 November 1995

'The Remarkable Story of Emily Anderson', *Galway Advertiser*, 8 February 2001

'Sanitation and Water Supply', *Galway Advertiser*, 5 October 1995

'The Sebastopol Trophies', *The Galway Vindicator*, 5 August 1857

'State of Galway', *The Galway Weekly Advertiser and Connaught Journal*, 9 December 1826

'Street Nuisances', *The Galway Vindicator*, 24 August 1861

'Synge the Snapper', *Galway Advertiser*, 14 July 2005

'Thomas Ashe Centenary to be marked in the city', *Galway City Tribune*, 3 June 1992

'To the Lighthouse', *Galway Advertiser*, 31 March 1994

'Tremendous and Frightful Hurricane', *The Galway Weekly Advertiser and Connaught Journal*, 12 January 1839

'Two Great Galway Athletes', *Galway Advertiser*, 3 August 1986

'A View from the Canal, 1903', *Galway Advertiser*, 25 September 1997

'Western Marathon', *The Connacht Tribune*, 9 October 1909

'What Good are the Watchmen?', *The Galway Vindicator*, 15 June 1861

'When Fire Destroyed Menlo Castle', *Galway Advertiser*, 9 March 2000

'Wolfe Tone, the Delightful Mrs. Martin and the Theatre in Kirwans Lane', *Galway Advertiser*, 26 November 1998

'Youngest Air Crash Victim Laid to Rest', *The Connacht Tribune*, 30 August 1958

Websites

'Anabaptists', www.questia.com/library/encyclopedia/anabaptists.jsp (June 2010)

'Forster (Blake Forster)', www.landedestates.ie/LandedEstates/jsp/estate-show.jsp?id=760 April 2010.

'History of the Victoria Cross', www.thevictoriacross.net/history/index.html (June 2009)

'More Tattoo Symbols and their Symbolism', www.tattoosymbol.com/articles/heart-dagger.html December 2010

'Richard Kirwan (Chemist, Mineralogist, Meteorologist and Geologist)', http://irishscientists.tripod.com/scientists/RICHARD.HTM (May 2010)

Riordan, C., 'Legends of St Nicholas Church Galway: The Mystery of Warden Bodkin's Hand', www.legendquest.ie (May 2010)

The World Book Encyclopaedia (1986)

'Concord, Battle of'
'First Continental Congress, The'
'Knights Templar'

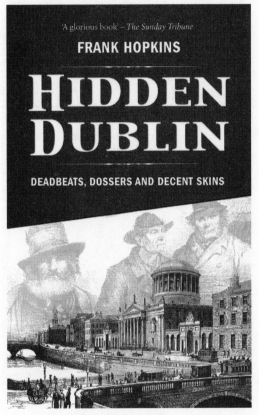

'A glorious book' – *The Sunday Tribune*

FRANK HOPKINS

HIDDEN DUBLIN

DEADBEATS, DOSSERS AND DECENT SKINS

978 1 85635 591 9

Criminal incidents, accidents, whippings, beatings, jail escapes and hangings were all part of Dublin's 'brilliant parade' in the eighteenth and nineteenth centuries, including actors, clergymen, scientists, politicians and rogues and rascals of every hue.

Hopkins describes the poverty, soup kitchens, food riots, street beggars and workhouses that were all a feature of Dublin life. He also introduces us to the weird, wonderful, and often strange customs and pastimes of Dubliners stretching back to the Middle Ages, such as the 'bearing of balls' annual parade by the city's bachelors and the ritual humiliation of would-be bridegrooms at the bullring.

www.mercierpress.ie

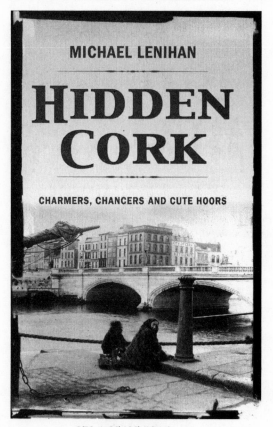

978 1 85635 686 2

In this collection, Michael Lenihan delves into the rich tapestry of Cork's history to reveal some of its most bizarre events and strangest characters. From quack doctor Baron Spolasco, to the outlaw Airt Ó Laoghaire, Cork has seen some eccentric, wonderful and even some downright nasty people.

With revelations of mass graves in Bishop Lucey Park, how Jonathan Swift was awarded the freedom of the city, stories of the Gas Works' strike and the trams of the city, *Hidden Cork* opens the door on history, dumps the boring bits and brings to life the flow of time through the streets of Cork.

www.mercierpress.ie

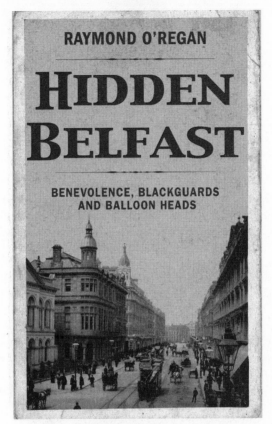

978 1 85635 683 1

Belfast has a history stretching back to AD 668 and like any modern-day city, it has seen its fair share of strange and fascinating characters and events. In *Hidden Belfast*, Raymond O'Regan explores the city's past to reveal some of its most interesting stories.

From Sir Arthur Chichester, founder of 'modern' Belfast, through the infamous spy Belle Martin, to Bruce Ismay, Managing Director of the White Star Line, who controversially ordered Harland and Wolff to reduce the number of lifeboats on the *Titanic* from forty-eight to sixteen, *Hidden Belfast* brings the more colourful parts of Belfast's history to life.

MERCIER PRESS

IRISH PUBLISHER - IRISH STORY

We hope you enjoyed this book.

Since 1944, Mercier Press has published books that have been critically important to Irish life and culture. Books that dealt with subjects that informed readers about Irish scholars, Irish writers, Irish history and Ireland's rich heritage.

We believe in the importance of providing accessible histories and cultural books for all readers and all who are interested in Irish cultural life.

Our website is the best place to find out more information about Mercier, our books, authors, news and the best deals on a wide variety of books. Mercier track the best prices for our books online and we seek to offer the best value to our customers, offering free delivery within Ireland.

Sign up on our website or complete and return the form below to receive updates and special offers.

www.mercierpress.ie
www.facebook.com/mercier.press
www.twitter.com/irishpublisher

Name: _____

Email: _____

Address: _____

Mercier Press, Unit 3b, Oak House, Bessboro Rd, Blackrock, Cork, Ireland